The
Successful
SECRETARY

The
Successful
SECRETARY

YOU, YOUR BOSS, AND THE JOB

Loren B. Belker

 A Division of American Management Associations

Library of Congress Cataloging in Publication Data

Belker, Loren B.
    The successful secretary.

    Includes index.
    1. Office practice. 2. Secretaries. I. Title.
HF5547.5.B415   651.3'741   81-66239
ISBN 0-8144-5683-9   AACR2

First Printing

For Marilyn,
an outstanding executive secretary
and my favorite sister

Preface

Many executives become dissatisfied with the performance of their secretaries. And although these high-powered managers have no difficulty communicating with peers, subordinates, or superiors, they don't do an effective job of communicating with their executive secretaries.

Unfortunately, there is a myth abroad in the land that a person holding the position of secretary knows just what is expected in the way of performance. It's as though instant knowledge goes with the title. Executives are busy people, and although it would be time well spent, they aren't going to block out two weeks of their lives to train a secretary in what is expected in the way of performance on *this* particular position. This book takes the place of such training by the executive. It contains the instructions I believe the secretary would receive if the executive could take the time to communicate the job's full requirements.

The person who has been an executive secretary for a decade may not need this book, especially if the working relationship between the executive and the secretary is such that the secretary knows exactly what is expected and how to meet those expectations.

In this country today, most executives are male and most executive secretaries are female. I do not condone such a situation, but it would be less than candid to deny its existence. Therefore to make it easier, I am not going to ask the reader to struggle through a book full of "he or she" and "his or her." The executive will be considered male and the secretary female. When that situation is no longer prevalent, future editions will reflect the change.

Loren B. Belker

Contents

x   **Contents**

1

The Executive's Attitude Toward the Secretary's Job

Most executives can tell you what they don't want. What they do want is harder for them to articulate. This makes it difficult for a secretary to know what is expected of her. The process is called on-the-job training. Unfortunately, many secretaries have to perform tasks or assume attitudes that displease the executive before they find out that's *not* what he wants.

Let's face it. One thing an executive wants from a secretary is someone who makes him look good. The secretary is an extension of the executive, and so is a part of an executive team. However, while he wants her to function as part of a team, he doesn't want a secretary to assume the authority of the office. This creates a problem, because it has the appearance of responsibility without the corresponding authority to get the job done. Most executives want the job done, but if push comes to shove, they don't want the secretary shoving. They'd rather have her back off and refer the matter to the executive for resolution. This kind of attitude creates many problems for the secretary, for she must take on the diplomatic skills usually reserved for people in the State Department. Tact and diplomacy are essential ingredients for a successful executive secretary. They substitute for authority.

An executive expects a secretary to work at her job. As

nonsensical as such a statement may sound, there are some executive secretaries who consider the job a soft spot where they can keep a low profile, especially if the executive must spend considerable time traveling. There are few things more irritating to any employer than to have an employee who waits to be told what to do. An executive secretary anticipates what needs to be done. At the outset, it may seem like an impossible task, but by the time you get to the end of this book, you should be more comfortable about it.

Everything an executive secretary does around the office reflects upon her boss. Although fortunately we have arrived at the point where people no longer "owe their soul to the company store," the fact remains that we can't completely separate our personal lives from our professional careers. What we are and what happens at the office impact upon our personal lives. The reverse is also true. Although we'd like to believe "what I do away from the office is no one's business," the fact is that what we do away from the office often affects the way we function at work.

An executive wants a secretary who is able to leave her personal problems outside the office door. Of course, some problems are so overwhelming they can't be left at home, but many lesser irritants can be kept away from the office.

It would be foolish to suggest that all executives view the secretary's job the same way. Obviously they don't. The knowledge required for a secretary's position may vary a great deal by the business you're in. A secretary working for an insurance company deals with different language and nomenclature than one employed by a company manufacturing water pumps. It's important for a secretary to learn the language of the business, be it on a formal or informal basis.

Some industries have basic educational courses available to member companies; others do not. But whether it's formal or casual, the language of the business should make sense to the secretary. The executive often can't or won't take the time to teach it to the new executive secretary, but he can suggest reading or other material that may be of some help. Of course if the secretary has been promoted from within, she is already familiar with the language.

Every executive agrees that a secretary should have a positive attitude. They don't want a Pollyanna who can't see a disaster staring her in the face, but they do want someone who generally likes the job and is cheerful about performing it. It's uncomfortable and plainly unpleasant to be around someone who is constantly complaining or can't find any pleasure in the job. All of us spend a very large part of our lives with our jobs, and executives are like any other human beings; they would rather work with people who are pleasant. No one expects a secretary to be "little Mary Sunshine" every day, but it's helpful if there are more sunshine-filled days than cloudy ones. Reverse the roles, and then decide which atmosphere you'd choose.

A calm and serene atmosphere is preferred. A secretary who comes unglued when half a dozen different developments all pop up at the same time will not last long with a busy top executive. There are enough job-related problems without having to calm down and compose an unraveled secretary. Everyone is familiar with the cliché, "If you can keep your head when others around you are losing theirs, you obviously don't understand the situation." You could rephrase that to read: "If you can keep your head when others around you are losing theirs, you're executive secretary material." The executive may not always keep his head, but if you keep your cool, it can only be helpful.

Most successful executives don't want a secretary who lacks courage. If his secretary won't stand up to him on important issues, she won't stand up to anybody else either. If she doesn't have convictions she won't be an effective team member. She must tread a delicate line that many secretaries have trouble recognizing.

A quality executive doesn't want a secretry who follows blindly. He wants someone who thinks. If she doesn't think, she won't help prevent errors, and she won't be effective. On the other hand, he doesn't want a secretary who makes every project a federal case, and he doesn't want a long harangue about the best way to approach every task. This balance is of critical importance, and you learn it by the "feel" of working with someone. You can even talk about it and come up with examples at both extremes, but the areas in the middle ground require judgment, which comes from experience. As one executive secretary told me, "You have to know how far you can push, before the push is considered a shove. My boss will accept a little pushing but won't stand still for any shoving."

Knowing where to find that line is crucial. Sometimes it's a wavy line. Many executives have occupational hobbies. They may concern little pet trivia that could be handled by the newest addition to the mail room, but if it's their hobby, don't mess with it. Sense has little bearing on the matter. Occupational hobbies are usually nonsensical. Often they are tasks that the executive brought with him from his former position in the company. They aren't logical, but they are accepted. If the executive for whom you're working has such hobbies, it won't take long to recognize them. *Leave them alone.*

The position of executive secretary is a supportive one, and support is what the executive expects. The more detail the secretary can assume, the more time the executive has for policy matters, for planning, and for the creative aspects of his job. An executive bogged down in detail is nothing more than an expensive clerk. The organization can't afford such extravagances. Most executives spend too much time on unproductive detail. Whenever any details are assumed by subordinates, executives have the opportunity to become more effective. The secretary is one of the subordinates to whom detail can and should be delegated.

An executive wants a secretary who realizes she has accepted a job, not a social position. There are many employees who believe that a hard day's work is beyond the call of duty. A secretary with such an attitude is in the wrong career. Some secretaries are underutilized and work at half pace. They get so used to it that they believe they are being overworked and abused when they are required to put in a full day's work. An executive wants a secretary who isn't afraid of a hard day's work.

Many executives looking for a quality secretary will investigate the background of an applicant (within the confines of current law and regulations) to see if the person has any history of accomplishment. A person who got so-so grades in school, who never moved into a position of leadership, who never earned a paycheck, who never knew the satisfaction and challenge of accomplishment will in all probability make a poor secretary.

Usually, top executives will look for someone from within their own organization who has been working as a secretary for a lower-level manager. They are going to look at performance and will reject a so-so performer. If you've been saying, "When I have a job worthy of my talents, then I'll do a good job," you'll never get the promotion. With that attitude, it's too late; the train has already left the station.

You will read a great deal about attitudes in this book. You can be the most talented secretary in the world, and if your attitude is bad, most executives won't put up with you. You can be less talented and have a super attitude and be considered a satisfactory performer.

This book is written with the assumption that the secretary has the fundamental skills the position requires. What counts is how you use these skills.

2

The Secretary's Attitude
Toward the Job and the Executive

If you feel that the position of secretary is demeaning, don't take the job. You'll be miserable, even if you perform well.

Much has been said lately about certain tasks secretaries are given that they consider the result of outdated, chauvinistic attitudes on the part of the executives they work for. I won't defend such attitudes, but they exist in the real world. What do you do about them?

If you feel that such requests as pouring coffee for the executive and guests, making dental and doctor appointments, and reminding the executive of his wife's and kids' birthdays are demeaning, you ought to settle these questions when you're being interviewed. If you're expected to do these things and you don't think you should, you have two choices. You can refuse the position, which reduces the question to how great a matter of principle it is with you, or you can explain why you don't believe it should be a part of the job and see if he wants to hire you anyway and remove these trivial aspects from the position. In fact, the executive has an obligation to make clear what his expectations are, but he may neglect to mention these.

I don't have much sympathy for a secretary who doesn't even broach the subject during the interview but becomes indignant about some of the tasks once she has the job. You could argue that such trivial or demeaning tasks shouldn't even have to be discussed. In this more enlightened world they shouldn't even be a factor. But we're talking about the real world, and therefore I believe it's best to clear the air before you take the job. An enlightened and flexible executive will understand what your concerns are. If he's rigid and a throwback to the ice age, aren't you better off finding out about it up front? You'd be unhappy working for a real clod, anyway. The interview is an opportunity for two people to determine mutual suitability.

You can't assume a younger executive will take a more enlightened view. That's not necessarily true. One reason you expect difficulty from older executives is the belief that they may have trouble breaking old habits. But flexibility is not necessarily a characteristic of youth or age.

If the secretarial candidate views the job as one of competition with the executive, she shouldn't take it. She should strive to help the executive to be more effective, not engage in a battle of wits or intelligence to prove she's as bright as he is and executive material herself. If you feel competitive, don't take an executive secretary position, because you'll be unhappy. Instead, get into a managerial training program.

Most people who enjoy an executive secretary's job prefer work that has structure and basic guidelines. They don't like "sink or swim" situations. Most secretaries like to see a beginning and an end to a task. They like benchmarks that enable them to know how they are doing. They like variety, but not panic situations that move them from one item to another without enough time to see anything to a conclusion. Secretaries need to feel appreciated for what they do. Of equal importance, they need to know what is expected of them.

Secretaries don't like indecisive executives, but they often misread the executive with whom they work. Too many people assume that you're either a decisive person or you're not. This isn't true. Some people can be very decisive about some problems and vacillate for an interminable amount of time on other matters. It may depend on the value system or the sense of priorities of the executive. I've known executives who could make a decision about spending thousands of dollars without much difficulty but would agonize for hours about having a performance appraisal with a subordinate who wasn't performing at a satisfactory level. This apparent contradiction isn't a contradiction at all. Not all executives are the same. If they were, you'd only need one in an organization.

Some executives can get rough with a vendor about an incorrect billing sent to the company, but hesitate to tell their secretaries they're overstaying their lunch hours. Executives often avoid tasks they'd be better off handling immediately. This doesn't mean they don't know any better. All of us have some things we consider unpleasant. Some of us tackle the unpleasant items early and get them out of the way. Others put them off and hope they'll go away.

Many secretaries expect tolerance and gentleness from their boss about mistakes and work deficiencies, but they become indignant when the executive makes a mistake that affects them. In extreme instances they expect typing mistakes in a letter to be excused but are annoyed if the boss decides to rewrite a paragraph.

Secretaries often expect an executive to be more even-tempered and keep to a much higher standard than themselves. Of course, it's better if neither the executive nor the secretary has wild mood swings, but no one is completely the same every day at the office, no matter how desirable that might be. Some secretaries treat their bosses like gods and behave as though their bosses should be able to walk on water, but if their bosses respond by believing them, they resent it.

Some management experts claim that the relationship between a boss and a secretary is similar to a marriage. There are some similarities, but there are dissimilarities, too. Executives and secretaries often spend more time together than a married couple. It's important, therefore, that they like each other. If one of them doesn't care much for the other's personality, the working relationship is going to be unpleasant for both people, and it ought to be terminated as quickly as possible. Life is too short to spend the major portion of your working hours with someone who drives you up the wall.

Every new secretary ought to be brought into a job on a probationary basis. Unfortunately for the secretary, the final decision is usually unilateral. If there is a ninety-day probationary period, for example, at the end of that time the executive decides whether or not the secretary should be retained. The secretary should also be given the opportunity to opt out of the arrangement.

Companies would have to change to make this possible. They'd have to provide a procedure that would allow the secretary to go back to a similar job to the one held before the probationary period. Granted, companies would also have to change their promotion procedures so that either person could back out of the deal without embarrassment or loss of face. Not only the executive has the chance to second-guess the decision. If the secretary doesn't like the arrangement she has only two choices. She can quit, or she can ask the personnel department for a transfer. Both parties should be able to back out of any promotion that doesn't work. From the company's point of view, it's an opportunity to retain a valuable employee. For the employee who likes the company and has benefits built up, it's a chance to stay on in a more suitable job. The Peter Principle may have come into play, with the secretary raised to a level of incompetence. It's better to adopt a system that allows her to stay where she'll be more productive rather than forces her to leave.

The difference between a satisfactory attitude and a poor one is often characterized by illness. Everyone wakes up some mornings feeling slightly under par. It's a gray area in which one employee will think, "I'm not sick enough to stay home," and another "I don't feel well enough to go to work." No reasonable executive wants someone to come to work when ill; but neither does he expect an employee to stay home to nurse a bad mood. There are also those who find religion when (and only when) it can be used to get out of work. Technically they are within their rights, but their attitude is all wrong. The amount of time spent in trying to get out of work would be better spent in figuring out how to be more productive.

Many younger people are not familiar with the phrase "soldiering on the job." It means taking the existing work and stretching it out to fill the time one must put in. Many people take an hour to do a fifteen-minute job. They assume they can manipulate their boss. If they really are more intelligent than the executive to whom they report, they'd be far better off working somewhere else. If they're mistaken, the mistake can be fatal.

If you're physically fragile, don't work as an executive secretary. It will be a constant source of irritation between you and your boss. You don't have to be as strong as a horse, but it helps. There are few things more irritating to an executive than an employee who's out frequently. It's even more irritating if that employee is his secretary, for whom dependability is a primary requisite.

Such ailments may be caused by stress. You may not like the job. Do you dread having the weekend come to an end? If you can't stand going back to work on Monday, you're in the wrong job. You don't have to look forward to Monday (although it would be a plus), but it's a bad sign if you dread it. It's no accident that most absences occur on Mondays and Fridays (except when they are paydays).

The employee who takes advantage of every technicality will make certain that she's "sick" right up to the maximum of the sick-leave benefits if the company has such a program. When the executive gets the feeling he's being taken advantage of, he'll check the attendance record. If there's a pattern, she's in trouble, because he'll start losing confidence in her. Loss of confidence in an executive secretary makes her useless. The result of the confidence crisis will be covered in another chapter.

Someone who regards a job as a necessary evil won't make a good executive secretary. There's nothing wrong with a job being fun. As a matter of fact, it helps. If you enjoy your job it won't tire you as much as if you hate it. Have you ever noticed that when you're with people you enjoy and engaged in an activity you all enjoy, the time passes quickly and you feel invigorated? Perhaps it's hoping for too much to expect such a feeling about your work, but the closer you can come to it the less it will seem like "just a job" and the less it will tire you. It is possible to feel invigorated from a productive day even when you also feel some physical impact from having worked hard for eight hours.

Absenteeism is more prevalent among younger employees. Obviously, physical condition and energy levels are not the problem. The difference has to be in attitude toward the job or boredom with the work. Even if we concede that younger people are stuck with the less interesting entry jobs, we also have to admit that increased responsibility often comes with experience and maturity. The fact that most successful executive secretaries are more mature is no accident. A younger person can be a successful executive secretary, but seasoning helps.

If you are thinking of becoming an executive secretary, examine your attitude honestly. How do you feel about work? Can you see yourself playing what is basically a supportive role? There's nothing wrong with wanting to be a star, but if that is your attitude, don't take a job as an executive secretary because you're going to compete with the person you're supposed to be supporting. The executive secretary is the ultimate example of a staff position.

3

Correspondence

A secretary used to be defined primarily as someone who takes shorthand and types letters. Today, people who grind out letters all day long usually work in stenographic pools.

The advertising campaigns of the nation's telephone companies would lead people to believe correspondence is an archaic way of conducting business. That's wishful thinking on the part of the ad agencies. Correspondence still plays, and will continue to play, an important role in the nation's business.

Although many executives use dictating equipment, every executive secretary should be able to take a letter in shorthand and to do it skillfully. Even the executive who uses dictating equipment will at times need shorthand skills from his secretary. For example, if an emergency develops right before the mail room is to close, and a letter must go out immediately, shorthand is often the answer. Or the executive may be out of the office and phone in several messages. Even if the messages are not letters to be transcribed, it helps a great deal for the secretary to record them in shorthand.

Some executives prefer dictating their letters to a secretary even though they are aware that dictating equipment is more efficient and less time-consuming. They may fear that dictating into a machine is so impersonal, the letter will end up sounding impersonal or cold. It takes more skill to dictate a warm letter to a piece of metal equipment than it does to a human being sitting across your desk. They may appreciate the fact that a secretary reacts to words she hears and transcribes to her steno pad. If something is unclear or she is not sure of a word, she can ask and clear up the ambiguity right on the spot. Another factor is that some people, executives included, play better to an audience, even an audience of one. There's a bit of ham in most of us.

The dictating style of executives varies a great deal. You will adapt to your boss's style. If you were tested on your shorthand before you were hired, it's obvious that your speed is sufficient, so if the executive appears to be going too fast for you at the outset, you can get him to slow down by saying, "Until I get used to your style of dictating, would you mind slowing down just a bit? I want to make certain I don't miss anything." This kind of approach will not bother him, because it indicates a desire on your part to transcribe the message correctly. That's a desirable trait in a secretary.

People don't talk the way they write. When people write something out in longhand or type a letter, they write in sentences. People don't speak in sentences in their everyday conversation. Body language and facial expressions play an important part in personal dialogue. You can't use them in correspondence. Most seasoned executives do dictate in complete sentences. Newer executives or a few who should know better will dictate the way they speak. If that happens, it's up to the secretary to translate the dictation into complete sentences. If she transcribes it word for word, he'll correct it when it's presented to him for signature, and she'll end up doing it over.

If the boss signs his mail without reading it and it contains errors, there's a possibility that both the boss and the secretary will look like fools in the eyes of the person receiving the correspondence. There's also the strong possibility that the boss will see a carbon of his letter when the reply comes in. If there's one thing an executive won't tolerate very long, it's a secretary who doesn't catch his grammatical errors and therefore causes him to look stupid.

When transcribing shorthand, you can often figure out what was intended. Go ahead and make the correction. If you're not sure, ask. An executive would rather have you ask than guess. His style will become obvious to you after you work with him for a while. The proper use of language is absolutely essential for an executive secretary. This is one area in which even the biggest ego won't object to your superior knowledge, because it's to his advantage. A secretary who types "roll" when "role" is required isn't going to survive long unless she's working for an executive who's willing to be patient and make corrections while she learns her trade. There are plenty of places where she can learn these basic skills. She should have them before she tries to become an executive secretary.

There are advantages to dictating equipment that we haven't discussed. The obvious one is that it doesn't tie up two people. While one person is dictating, the other one can perform some other task. The secretary doesn't have to be present while the executive is dictating. If he wants to come in on the weekend to catch up on his correspondence, the secretary doesn't have to be present with her stenographic pad. Such an arrangement can save money. With the availability of quality, portable dictating equipment, the executive can dictate while away from the office and even while traveling.

When an executive asks his secretary to use her shorthand only in emergency situations, the skill may deteriorate. It would behoove him to dictate enough letters to her to keep her skills sharp. If he doesn't think of it, there's nothing wrong with her asking him periodically to dictate directly to her. A secretary can also work on her shorthand skills when her boss is out of town, but has left several "belts" or "records" of dictation. Instead of transcribing the dictation from the earphones to the typewriter, she can set the playback equipment at a normal voice speed and take shorthand from the voice coming through the earphones. She can then type the letter from the shorthand and read it back after it's typed, checking herself against the dictaphone. This method enables her to keep her shorthand skills sharp without impinging on the executive's time. Many experienced secretaries also take dictation from the radio.

How you handle incoming mail will depend on your organization's mail system. Some mail rooms open all mail except letters or packages marked "personal" or "confidential." In other companies any mail addressed to a specific person is sent on to that person still sealed.

How the executive prefers his mail handled plays an important part in the system. Some executives want to open all mail personally addressed to them. Others will have the secretary open all mail, even letters marked "personal." Still others have their secretaries open all mail except what is marked "personal" or "confidential."

Once the mail is opened, the secretary should scan it to see what file needs to be pulled in order for the executive to process the matter or handle it with thoroughness. It's frustrating for an executive to read an incoming letter that refers to the executive's previous mail and not to have the pertinent file attached. We will cover a simplified advance file system in a later chapter.

Inexperienced secretaries make the mistake of thinking that the only file they need to put with an incoming letter is any previous correspondence the executive may have had on the same subject or with the same person. If Fred Jones writes about the Chicago lease, it isn't enough to find out if there's been any previous correspondence with Fred Jones. You also need to look for any correspondence about the Chicago lease, plus the lease file itself.

Try to anticipate every bit of information the executive

might need in order to take the next action or to resolve the matter. Then attach it, always putting the latest letter on top. Although it may be so obvious it doesn't need to be mentioned, I would just like to remind secretaries that the overwhelming majority of executives want files maintained with the latest information on top. The oldest item should be at the bottom of the file.

How executives receive their mail is important to some of them. The volume of mail they receive is a factor. When we talk of mail, we're referring to both mail received from outside the office and mail routed internally from other people in the same company. Some executives prefer just one in-box where they can review everything that has come in that day. Others may have two or more in-boxes, and will have you separate the mail into several categories. The first box would be for urgent matters, the second for important but not urgent mail, the third for advertisements, flyers, or other mail where delay won't have an adverse impact.

A secretary must use judgment. For example, she may know that her boss looks at all mail in the first two boxes within a day of getting back into town after a business trip. The flier announcing the company cocktail party might ordinarily go into the third box, but if the RSVP deadline is within three days of the boss's return to the office, he had better see the invitation while he still can make his reservation. So just because advertisements and fliers ordinarily go into the third in-box doesn't mean she can put everything of that nature in there without any thought.

If you were to survey all the executives in the country and ask for their top five complaints about secretaries, the failure to exercise commonsense judgment would certainly rank among those top five. Most executives have just one in-box either because they don't get much mail or because they don't trust their secretary's judgment to establish the category of the mail. If your boss asks you to set priorities on his incoming mail and you're in doubt, it's always best to err toward the urgent side than toward the unimportant end of the scale. It's simple for him to toss a letter into the less important tray, but if he fails to see an important memo on time you may both be in trouble.

Few executives will allow a secretary to throw away junk mail, because you two may not have the same definition of junk. There may be something in that pile of mail he'll want to see. Contrary to popular opinion, not everything categorized as junk mail is junk. The amount of sales made each year by mail indicates catalog sales are a thriving business.

Some mail marked "personal" or "confidential" has to be handed back to the secretary for the file to be pulled. Although the sender may regard it as "personal" or "confidential," the recipient may not consider it special. There are executives, especially those who travel a great deal, who have their personal mail come to the office. That way, they don't have to go to the post office to stop and start their mail each time or have mail accumulate in their mailbox and let people know they are out of town. Such personal mail shouldn't be mixed in with company mail. If there isn't a special box for it, it should be placed on the executive's desk. And it should never be opened by the secretary, unless she is specifically requested to do so.

Now let's discuss the quality of the correspondence coming from the executive's dictation and the secretary's typing. That letter leaving your office is a direct reflection on the organization and the executive whose name appears at the bottom of it. As a result, it should be flawless.

Many secretaries consider "liquid paper" a great time saver, whereas their bosses believe it makes a letter look like Tom Sawyer's whitewashed fence. Going over an occasional character with this correcting fluid may be acceptable, but modifying entire lines is unacceptable. A great deal of correcting fluid on a letter is an adverse reflection on the professionalism of the secretary. An exception might be made when a letter is being typed for photocopying and the original isn't being distributed. The white paint correction ordinarily can't be detected on a photocopy.

The type of margins and the format of letters may vary from office to office, and it may even vary from one executive to another. If you're not sure of what is expected, look at some previous correspondence or ask your boss how he likes his letters set up. If the executive's title is shown on the letterhead, you need not repeat it at the end of the letter after his name, unless he prefers it that way. Some people will add the title only if the letter goes to a second page. Some people believe there is a right way, but I think that it's a matter of personal preference.

Speaking of second sheets, the quality and weight of the second sheet should be identical to those of the first page. The purpose of having quality letterheads is defeated if the second page of the letter is on paper that came from the local thrift shop. Carbon copies for the file need not be on high-quality paper, unless the file is going to receive an inordinate amount of wear.

Once the letter is completed, different methods can be used for file management and for presenting the letter to the executive for signature. One method is to lay the entire file on the executive's desk with the newly dictated letter and any enclosures on top. He can then read the letter, check the enclosures, and sign the correspondence. The advantage of this method to the secretary is that she maintains the integrity of the file. The boss doesn't have to wonder if everything is attached. He can see it all. The other method is for the secretary to retain the file and just give the boss the letters to be signed.

Some companies have automatic sealing machines in the mail room where mail is sealed and then run through the postage meter. If you're working for an executive who deals with many sensitive or confidential matters, you ought to seal the letters before they leave your work area.

Many confidential pieces of correspondence are inner office memos. The confidentiality of this correspondence must be protected. The secretary shouldn't leave these letters lying on top of her desk, where inquisitive eyes can steal a few glances. They shouldn't be left in the typewriter when she leaves her desk either. There are always "secret agents" who know how to gather grist for the rumor mill. These are the people who have learned to stand in front of your desk and decipher the letter lying on top because they're adept at reading upside down. We'll cover the confidentiality responsibility of an executive secretary in a later chapter, but it's important to handle correspondence in a careful manner. Secretaries of top executives are prime targets of rumor mongers.

When sending inner office memos to other executives in the office, put them in envelopes unless they are so innocuous that your boss wouldn't mind if they ended up on the company bulletin board. Any message that goes through the routing system without being in a sealed envelope is likely to become common knowledge throughout the organization.

An executive secretary may become so matter-of-fact about confidential matters that she becomes careless. Without being privy to some of the boss's private conversations she may not be aware of the sensitive nature of a project. Carelessness could be devastating. Sensitivity may vary by company or industry. The rule ought to be "If in doubt—don't." During World War II, one patriotic slogan was "A slip of the lip could sink a ship." For the executive secretary, a slip of the lip could sink a project (and your job). A secretary should treat all of her boss's correspondence as confidential.

The letters you prepare for the executive are a direct reflection on both of you. Take pride in the quality of letters that bear your initials. Don't settle for second best or good enough to get by. You can't take any pride in being mediocre.

4

The Telephone

The letters that go out over an executive's name create an impression. So does the telephone that is answered on his behalf. Outside callers are usually greeted first by a switchboard operator. The quality of that person's voice is an important part of the first impression people receive of the organization.

The first impression people get of an executive is when his phone is answered. A few executives still answer their own phones, usually when their calls have gone through a switchboard. You can almost never dial an executive directly and have him answer the phone. He doesn't answer his own phone because he wants to be able to control his telephone time. If the calls are screened, as they come in, the executive has better control over how and with whom he spends time on the phone.

Although most executives dial their own calls, when time is pressing and a great number of long-distance calls are made, a busy executive may want his secretary to place his calls for him. The mistake is made when the party being called comes on the line and is asked by the secretary, "Mr. Jones, will you hold for Mr. Smith?" This should never be done. Mr. Jones may consider his time just as valuable as Mr. Smith's. Smith wants to talk to Jones, so Mr. Jones should not be inconvenienced by waiting until Mr. Smith can come to the phone.

When I am asked if I will hold for Mr. Smith, my answer, especially if it's a busy day and I don't know who Mr. Smith is anyway, is likely to be, "No, I won't." I then hang up. Of course I don't do it if it's somebody I want to talk to and I wouldn't be stupid enough to hang up on my boss. On the other hand, no boss ever did that to me. The point is that even if I dare not hang up, it's irritating to sit with a dead line waiting for Mr. Hotshot to pick up the phone. "Rank has its privilege" is still true, but you must consider the reaction of the person on the other end of the line. It may be necessary for some executives to have their calls placed for them, but they ought to be on the line when the person being called comes on the phone.

Some companies are adopting what is sometimes called a "closed period." During a closed period no one in the office calls anyone on the phone, visits, or holds any meetings. I'm sure the idea came about when some executive went to the office on a weekend, only to be amazed at how much was accomplished in two or three hours. In analyzing why, this person suddenly realized that the reason had to do with no interruptions from the telephone, people coming into the office, or meetings. Office productivity can be increased quite dramatically by such a procedure. Some organizations do modify the procedure to take outside calls from customers and clients. This is a reasonable modification, because the companies wouldn't exist without their customers.

How does a secretary answer the call that comes in during a closed period? If your company has a closed period, you can assume that only outside calls will be coming through the switchboard, so you take the call and put it through to your boss. If it's an inside call the executive may feel pretty sure that the call is important or the caller wouldn't have violated the closed-period concept. If callers constantly violate the spirit of the concept, the executive will take care of it.

How should a secretary answer the phone? A pleasant tone of voice is essential. Any harshness will create a bad impression. People can't control the kind of voice they were given, but they can practice sounding pleasant, efficient, and businesslike. You shouldn't go to the other extreme, so that you sound as if you're answering the phone for the Aphrodite Massage Parlor.

Getting in the habit of smiling when you answer the phone will do wonders for your tone of voice. This isn't easy when you're in the middle of a million things and the last thing you want is one more interruption; but the person calling doesn't know it's a bad time to call and shouldn't be snapped at. A small mirror with a stand-up bracket placed next to the phone will be helpful as a training device. The problem with leaving it on your desk permanently is that people will think you are narcissistic.

Another way you can improve your telephone voice is to have it recorded by a friend. A small suction device with a contact microphone can be bought at almost any sound or stereo shop for a few dollars. It plugs into the microphone connection on a cassette recorder. Have your friend call you several times. While recording on the cassette answer the phone in various ways. Make a note of what you were thinking each time. You can then hear what you sound like to others over the telephone. Otherwise, you can only guess at the impression you make or take your friends' word for it. Friends are unlikely to tell you if your voice is unpleasant because they won't want to hurt your feelings. They may tell you you sound great when you sound terrible. No matter how badly you sound or think you sound on the phone, you can improve your phone voice enough to make it pleasant to anyone on the other end.

If your company has a switchboard, you need not give the company's name when answering the phone. All you need to say is, "Mr. Smith's office." You don't need to add, "Mary speaking." Whoever is calling Mr. Smith wants to know he or she has reached his number, and probably doesn't care if Mr. Smith's secretary's name is Mary, Gertrude, or Penelope. If the person is calling Penelope on Mr. Smith's line, he or she already knows you're Penelope. If you have two lines and your line rings then it's proper to say, "Penelope speaking." Some people insist on adding the word "speaking" after their names. It's all right, but it isn't necessary. Giving your name proves you're on the line. If you're in a small office and you answer all incoming calls, give the name of the company. However, most executive secretaries do not double as switchboard operators.

When you answer the phone for your boss, never ask, "Who's calling, please?" This says to the person on the other end of the line, "Well, if you're important enough I may put you through." It's preferable to say, "May I tell him who's calling?" You receive the same information, but you've asked for it in a more diplomatic way.

Many secretaries have difficulty in knowing how to answer the phone when the executive is not in the office. When a phone call comes before he arrives in the morning you don't say, "He's not here yet." Instead you should say something like, "Mr. Smith isn't in his office right now. May I have him call you?" It's none of the caller's business whether or not Mr. Smith has come in yet. Mr. Smith may have a civic breakfast meeting, or he may be late. One of the responsibilities of an executive secretary is to help him to do his job more effectively, and this includes making him look good.

When you leave phone messages for the executive always include the phone number. Don't assume he knows it or that he has it in his address book. Ask the other party for the number and write it down. It is frustrating for a person to come back to his office to be greeted by a dozen phone memos with no phone numbers noted. Occasionally, when you ask for a phone number, the caller will say, "Oh, he knows it." Thank the caller, but go to the executive's address book, look up the number, and write it down. One of your functions is to save your boss's time. One reason many executives have their secretaries place phone calls is so they don't waste time looking up phone numbers. Granted, with some executives, having a secretary dial phone calls is an ego trip, but most do it to save time.

Some employees spend an inordinate amount of time visiting on the telephone. Remember, in an office a telephone is meant to be an instrument of industry and commerce. It's not there as a social instrument for the secretary or anyone else. No reasonable executive will object to an occasional personal phone call as long as the privilege is not abused, but extensive (or long-distance) use of the telephone by the secretary is inexcusable.

Sometimes it would be helpful if certain files were pulled and put with the phone messages. You won't be able to decide on the appropriateness of doing this until you're well acquainted with your boss's work habits. In the early days of the job, you might ask him if there are any files he would like pulled before he returns his phone calls.

There should always be two pads by his telephone. One is for him to make notes while talking on the phone. The other is for him to write notes to his secretary. There should be a buzzer device either on the phone or somewhere in his office that can be heard at your desk. While he's on the phone, he might buzz you. When you enter you find he's on the phone, but he could write a note to you that says, "Rutherford file" meaning, "I need that file for this call."

The executive might arrange for signals on the buzzer system. For instance, one ring could mean come in, and two rings bring your steno pad with you. Often such buzzer systems are available as part of the telephone system.

5

The Daily Meeting

An effective way to begin each workday is with a meeting between the executive and the secretary. Whether the meeting is formal or informal depends on the people involved. Important misunderstandings can be avoided if both people know what is expected and what is to be done. One can't blame a secretary if she has what she believes are three equally important tasks to perform and she chooses the third, only to find out later that the executive considered the second more important.

Also, the executive should not tell the secretary only what he wants done that day and in what order. He should let her know what his plans are. Many executives become quite irritated when they ring for their secretaries and receive no answer. They don't know where their secretaries are or when they'll be back. What they don't realize is that their secretaries face the identical problem. They take off and don't let their secretaries know where they're going to be. When an emergency comes up, the secretaries have no idea where to try to reach their bosses. Executives must be aware that effective communication is a two-way street.

The daily meeting can vary greatly, depending on the kind of business you're in. Some executives believe the meeting is more effective if held at the end of the day, and the time is used to establish the plan for the next day. I disagree for several reasons.

Most offices are quite hectic toward the end of the day. You're trying to get out that rush letter. Your boss and you both may be tired from a hard day's work and without much energy. If the day was hectic, you're both probably interested primarily in ending it and going on your respective ways. The last thing you're in the mood to do is to draw up plans for tomorrow's nervous breakdown. I believe there's an advantage to letting one day wind to its conclusion independent of the next.

However, for some executives and their secretaries the daily meeting at the end of the day may work fine. If it's working, don't change it. The one time it's handy is when the executive is going to be out of the office the next day. He'll often give last-minute instructions. Some of these last-minute instructions may be necessary. I still feel, though, that if he's going to be out of the office on Friday, there is likely to be a more thorough discussion of what needs to be done if it's discussed in detail at a Thursday morning meeting.

The meeting between the executive and the secretary should be a dialogue, not a monologue. The executive may start out discussing items he has on his mind, but when he's finished, he should be prepared to listen to a discussion of work requirements from the secretary. An executive can overlook an important item if he doesn't open the daily meeting to two-way communication.

An executive usually knows what is going on in an organization; that is, he knows what is supposed to be going on. Very few executives have instant access to the grapevine. Most secretaries do. It's important for an executive to know what's really going on; informal communication can't be ignored.

I don't mean to imply that the secretary should become a stool pigeon and violate the confidences of friends, but the daily meeting can be the basis for effective communication. If the executive believes a certain company program has broad-based support in the company and the secretary knows that people are only paying lip service to it and actually believe the program is a farce, that is vital information for an executive to have.

Where should the secretary draw the line? Many people in an organization tell an executive secretary things precisely because they want them to get to the executive. It's a simple and usually safe way to get a message to an executive without having to make a federal case out of it. By keeping it to herself, the secretary may be thwarting the intention of the person who gave her the information in the first place. Some secretaries may feel they should not be used to get messages to the executive. Good judgment should prevail.

There are items floating through the grapevine that the executive should know. Usually he can be told without confidences being violated. The secretary doesn't have to say, "Mary Ryan thinks the company's new vacation program is rotten." In the first place, if Mary Ryan is the only person who feels that way, there may not be a problem. However, if eight people who have lunch together all agree, either there is a problem with the new vacation program, it hasn't been explained very well, or both.

Some people gripe for its therapeutic value. It is a way of life for them. An experienced secretary soon learns to separate the chronic gripers from people with genuine concerns.

There are items that clearly cross the line and must be communicated. For example, if the secretary learns through the grapevine that someone is stealing from company inventory out of the shipping department, she is obligated to tell the executive about it. For a secretary to have such knowledge and keep it to herself could make her an accessory to a crime. The secretary needs to know that she can discuss almost anything with the executive and that he will handle sensitive information with a great deal of discretion. This topic will be covered more fully in the chapter on confidentiality.

A good way to begin the daily meeting is to review any items of business left over from the day before. On Mondays you might review the previous week. The daily meeting can give purpose to the day. It's not a unilateral goal-setting device. It can work for both parties. The secretary should list her goals for the day. The executive will often do the same. Making a list may seem childish, but it's the results that count. The list is always there to glance at during the day, and helps you to keep your eye on the ball. In addition, there's satisfaction derived from drawing a line through the goals as they're reached. At the end of the day, you never wonder what you accomplished. It's there on the pad for you to see. The items that are left constitute a beginning list for tomorrow's meeting.

The appointments on the executive's calendar should be reviewed at the daily meeting. Many secretaries are faithful about getting all the executive's appointments on his calendar, but they often neglect to put his appointments on their own desk calendar. As a result, when someone calls wanting to know if your boss is likely to be available at 2 o'clock, you can't answer without going in his office and looking at his calendar. If he has someone in his office, you may not be able to find out for some time. When you put a committee appointment on his calendar, you should also mark it on your own calendar.

It is a good idea to compare desk calendars at the daily meeting. The executive may very well say, "My appointment with Phil Jones for 2:00 P.M. today has been canceled. I saw Phil last night and we have that matter all settled." The secretary might say, "The president's secretary called late yesterday afternoon to tell us the finance committee scheduled for 11:00 this morning has been changed to 1:30 this afternoon. You were scheduled to visit with data processing at that time."

The secretary can delete the appointment with Phil Jones from her calendar and reschedule the visit to data processing. Full communication between the secretary and the executive will avoid many problems. You've heard it said of someone, "He's so inept he could foul up a two-car parade." It's amazing how inept the communication between an executive and a secretary can be. The daily meeting goes a long way toward solving communication problems.

After the secretary and her boss work together for a while, she will begin to understand his priorities. Some executives have a fetish about answering their correspondence quickly. Others feel two weeks is a prompt response. The secretary must adopt the executive's sense of priorities as her own.

We briefly mentioned the executive's travel time or other times away from the office. The daily meeting may need to be extended when the executive is planning a trip that will keep him away from the office for several days. The secretary should not feel that when her boss is away she can play. If she does, she probably won't last long. She has to assume that her boss got where he is because he's pretty smart and she won't be able to fool him. Besides, other executives see how she functions in his absence. If she's taking advantage of it, one of them will probably say something to him. If the executive suspects her of goofing off while he's gone, he may ask one of his friends to keep an eye on her. If you have to be watched, you are not executive secretary material. Sooner or later, it will catch up with you and you'll be terminated.

A secretary should make a list of projects to do if she ever gets the time. Few secretaries will admit it to anyone, but there are times when they don't have enough to do. If this never happens to you, you're either tremendously overworked or poorly organized. When things are slow, a "Someday, I'm gonna" file is useful. One project always in my "Someday, I'm gonna" file is to purge my files. I don't get to it as often as I should, and I can't delegate it to my secretary because she wouldn't necessarily feel the way I do about what's expendable and what's not.

The point is to have useful work to do when you have caught up with all high-priority items. Of course, many secretaries are busier than ever when their bosses are away, because some of the executives' responsibilities fall on their shoulders.

Some executives set priorities for their work in three categories: "emergencies," "must get to soon," and "no hurry," although most separate their work into two divisions: "right away" and "can wait." I believe the three categories provide more flexibility and can be disposed of more accurately. During the daily meeting, you can't assume that the order of discussion is necessarily the order of priority. At the end of the discussion, it is helpful to say, "May I read this list of projects I've written down to make certain I have all of them? And if this is not the order you want, I can renumber them in the order you do want." If the executive has no objections to the way you have the projects listed, it's fair to assume the order is okay.

The secretary must maintain an attitude of flexibility. Even the best-designed plans for the day can be shot down with emergencies that can't be anticipated. The list shows what was not done. It is then taken to the next morning's meeting and becomes the point of discussion for the next day.

The daily meeting isn't going to solve all the problems the executive and the secretary face, but it goes a long way toward establishing the priorities of the day. When items come up during the day that must be done immediately, be sure to add them to your list. It shows you what's to be done, but it also shows you what you complete. If ten items were on the list coming out of the daily meeting, and at the end of the day the first ten items remain, but lines are drawn through items 11 through 17, it's obvious that many unexpected matters came up.

Some people maintain these daily lists in a file. That may only give you another file to purge some day. Once a list has been used as the basis for the next day's meeting, there's some satisfaction in throwing it away.

Not all executives go for daily meetings, because they seem too formal an approach to management style. However, they should try them for a couple of weeks. I believe they'll find the meetings improve the productivity of both the executive and the secretary.

6

Office Hours

The inclusion of a chapter on office hours may seem un-necessary to the reader. After all, everyone should be there when the office day begins and shouldn't leave before quitting time. But it's not that simple. Of course, the secretary must be at the office on time and must not leave before the office day ends, because she is a reflection on the executive she works for and on the company itself.

Many secretaries don't realize that an executive's day may be considerably longer than their eight-to-five regimen. The other possibility is that he is taking advantage of the rank-has-its-privileges (RHIP) syndrome. The executive is responsible for his own office behavior; some junior executives who resent the RHIP of senior executives avail themselves of those same privileges when they achieve senior executive status. In any case, the secretary is responsible only for her own behavior, not that of her boss.

It is safe to say that even if the executive comes into the office an hour after it opens, with few exceptions he is putting in much longer hours than the secretary or junior executives may realize. For example, although a secretary may do volunteer work for her favorite charity when it pleases her, the executive who was attending a civic committee meeting that lasted until 11:30 P.M. was probably asked to be on that committee because of his position with your company and probably felt obliged to accept for the same reason. A senior executive cannot shut off his corporate responsibilities when he walks out the office door. He represents the company in almost everything he does.

Many secretaries and other company employees envy the travel some executives do for the organization. They seem to go to exciting places and do exciting things. Sometimes that's true. More often the travel they undertake for the company is boring and physically tiring. Getting into O'Hare Airport a half hour after your connecting flight has departed and having to spend the night at a nearby hotel without your baggage isn't a glamorous way of life. Most of the excitement of executive travel lasts about six months.

Many executives would gladly give up a portion or all of their next salary increase for a year of evenings at home with their families.

Although the secretary may work forty hours a week plus some occasional overtime, it's not at all unusual for an executive to put in sixty or seventy hours a week, especially when you include travel time. Of course, he's well compensated for what he does, but presumably you are also fairly compensated for your production.

The fact of the matter is that an executive's workweek consists of a great deal more than his office hours. It is also true that his hours and his output are his superior's concern, not his secretary's. When she resents the fact that she sometimes come into the office an hour before her boss, the secretary must bear in mind the difference in responsibilities. She must also remember that she is responsible to him, not vice versa.

There is a temptation for some employees not to get heavily involved in the day's activity until the boss arrives. Your responsibilities are the same whether he's there or not. You shouldn't need a watchman. Even if you can't have your daily meeting until the executive arrives, there are many things you can do. Until you have your daily meeting, you're still working on yesterday's list of things to do.

Some secretaries believe that their boss's rank allows them special privileges. If such privileges are specifically given to the secretary, that's one thing, but for the secretary to assume privileges because of the status of her boss is presumptuous. If the other secretaries have one hour for lunch, you shouldn't take an hour and fifteen minutes even if you can get away with it. Even though others might not say anything to you about it, people will resent it. Some will resent you anyway because of your job; there's no sense in justifying their feelings by inappropriate action on your part.

Some executive secretaries assume small prerogatives that their associates resent and that don't rightly belong to them. For example, when the executive is out of town or on vacation, an executive secretary may not pay much attention to getting to work on time, take a longer lunch hour, or go out for a little shopping in the middle of the day. This is perceived as dishonesty and it is. The only thing that would make it honest would be if the executive approved it in advance, and I doubt if most thoughtful executives would approve such behavior if they realized the impact upon others in the organization.

Executives and executive secretaries live in a corporate goldfish bowl and must conduct themselves accordingly. Enough of what happens around an office is misinterpreted without anyone deliberately setting out to irritate others. An executive secretary who pays strict attention to office hours, coffee breaks, and lunch hours sets a good example for others in the office. If the secretary to Mr. Smith considers it important to get to work on time, her attitude will have a positive impact on others in the organization. Conversely, if the secretary to a high-ranking officer doesn't have to observe the rules, other people may feel the rules aren't considered important, or she wouldn't get away with it. You may not believe your behavior has an impact on others in the organization, but it does, so your strict adherence to office hours is important.

Office hours include attendance. Companies keep attendance records and it's embarrassing for an executive to look at these records and see that his secretary has an attendance record far worse than the company average. No reasonable executive would react negatively if his secretary's attendance was worse than the company average because she was out of the office for six weeks to have surgery. What we're talking about are a plethora of minor complaints that sometimes keep people at home. As we mentioned earlier, the attitude of an employee has a tremendous impact on his or her attendance.

7

The Advance File

I am constantly amazed at the number of executives and secretaries who don't have an advance file system. Such a system is essential in an office. Some companies have elaborate systems, and for some executive secretaries, they are as basic as notes on a daily calendar.

But even if companies have elaborate advance file systems, their executives don't use them, because they don't want their correspondence exposed to everyone in the file room. The executive's files are maintained either in his office, under lock and key, or in the secretary's work area.

It is fundamental to say that a file consisting of data on a given topic or correspondence with one person or one company should be kept with the most recent item at the top. Once, while visiting a district office, I had the opportunity to examine the file system. This system had been established by the secretary in an office in which she represented the entire office secretarial and clerical staff. The manager of the office couldn't be bothered with such mundane matters as file organization. His instructions to the secretary had been, "You set up the files any way you like. All I ask is that you be able to find things when I need them."

This secretary had an exotic approach to file maintenance. Instead of getting a file together by person or subject she established the files by origin of the writer. There were files for letters from the clients to the district office; from the district office to the client; from the district office to the home office about the client; from the home office to the district office about the client; and even for mail to or from all other sources about the client. That made five separate file possibilities for John Smith, so when the district manager wanted to see the John Smith file, the secretary would ask the ridiculous question, "Where did the letter come from?" If he wanted the complete John Smith file, he had to search five separate file folders.

In this case, since it was a very small district office, this secretary could usually find whatever the district manager was searching for. The house of cards came tumbling down when she went on vacation and the district manager came unglued trying to find things.

As ridiculous as the foregoing is, the fault doesn't lie with the inventive secretary. The fault lies with the district manager who had no idea what kind of filing system he wanted or needed.

There are executives who don't want to be bothered with such details, but they should control the kind of file system that is established for their files and correspondence. If they have no other interest, the ability to find a file on a weekend or when the secretary's gone ought to be sufficient motivation.

One of the main objectives of an advance file system is to make certain some action that needs to be taken in the future is not overlooked. There are two integral parts of a simplified advance file system. The first part is the card file. This advance card file can consist of either 3 × 5 cards or 5 × 8 cards fitted into an appropriate box that sits either on the secretary's desk or inside one of its top drawers. Inside the box are three sets of daily cards numbered one to thirty-one, twelve monthly cards, plus another card labeled "next year." If you're going to put something on advance for more than the ninety-three days for which you have specific cards, you can put it in the month involved and move it into the exact day when the first day of that month arrives. The second part of the advance file is an active pending file that is alphabetical and is kept close to the secretary's desk.

Let's see how this simplified system works. Let's assume you're working in a district office of an insurance company. In our example, John Smith, a policyholder, requests a policy loan that must be secured from the home office. When you type up the letter requesting the loan, a copy is made for Mr. Smith's file, which is maintained in a manila folder. Since Mr. Smith's folder is in the permanent file, it is pulled. If there is no file for Mr. Smith, one must be established.

You then determine how long it should take to get an answer from the home office. For the sake of smooth follow-up, it's better to assume too short rather than too long a period.

You estimate you should have a response from the home office in ten days. If the request is sent on January 10, you would mark your file copy of the letter January 20, preferably in the upper-right-hand corner and in pencil. You use pencil because if you need to photocopy the file copy, the pencil marks are easily erased. It's a detail, but it may be important when neatness counts.

At the same time, you make a 3 × 5 or a 5 × 8 card, depending on the size you've chosen. Type or write the insured's name in the upper-left-hand portion of the card (last name first). To the right of the card, pencil in "January 20." Now you go to the box containing the advance cards and drop the card behind the twentieth date in January.

On January 20, you are ready to pull all your advance cards for that date. Among them is the card for John Smith. This leads you to John Smith's file in the alphabetic pending file in or near your desk. Once the Smith file is pulled, you can see at a glance that you're waiting for a policy loan check from the home office. Depending on what arrangement you've made with your boss, he may want you to handle all first follow-ups, processing the second follow-up himself or expecting you to write a letter for his signature. If you follow up and readvance the file, you repeat the process.

Now let's show how the file and advance card are treated when the response is received from the home office. Let's assume the check comes in from the home office on January 25 (after you've followed up and readvanced to January 30). When you open the mail, you see the loan check made payable to John Smith. If you handle a large volume of mail, it's unlikely you'd remember the file is on advance to January 30.

You go to the pending file and alphabetically pull the John Smith file. When you look at the Smith file, it becomes obvious the action requested has now taken place, and in the upper-right-hand corner you see the penciled date of January 30. This tells you it's on advance to January 30. You then go to the advance card box and pull the Smith card from the January 30 slot and throw it away. If your office is being frugal, you can draw a line through Smith's name and the advance date and use the card again.

The file is now ready to be closed (after you send Mr. Smith's loan check to him). Move Smith from the pending file back to the permanent file. The file is then closed until the next action involving Mr. Smith comes to the surface.

An advance file opens up all kinds of possibilities for a secretary to show the executive how efficient she is. For example, she can use it for birthday reminders. More and more executives are sending birthday cards to business associates, and the advance file can be used for this purpose. The secretary can have the matter come up soon enough for mailing. She could have the executive sign a month's supply of cards at the beginning of the month. That's the last he would need to see of it, because it would work automatically from that point forward.

The secretary can use the advance file system for all kinds of reminders, including anniversaries and meetings. For meetings, the advance file could be used to make certain the proper materials are prepared and ready. Letters that are sent on some kind of regular basis can be triggered from the advance file system. Anything that must happen at some point in the future can be helped by this simple system. One of its greatest advantages is that you stay on top of all situations. If people are supposed to have reports to your boss by a certain date, you can put that date in your advance file, and if the reports aren't there, you can either tell the executive or call and inquire as to their whereabouts.

This kind of attention to reports is particularly useful if you have associates similar to those of a friend of mine. If he suspected people weren't paying much attention to reports he furnished, he'd simply withhold them for several days to see if anyone missed them. Sometimes he'd hold them for two months before anyone noticed. This was his method to call attention to the preparation of unnecessary reports.

One of the advance file's greatest values is for answers to important correspondence. If a letter isn't answered in a reasonable amount of time, that fact comes to your attention and you can do something about it. If payments are due by a certain date, you could use the advance file to alert you. However, this kind of responsibility lies with the accounting department in a larger firm or the bookkeeper or accountant in a small business.

If you don't have an advance file, by all means establish the simple system we've described. After thirty days, you'll wonder how you ever operated without it. But its greatest recommendation is that it makes you more efficient and an invaluable assistant to the executive with whom you are associated.

8

The Art of Anticipation

When we discuss the art of anticipation, we are talking about a concept that becomes instinctive after you work with an executive for a while. The art of anticipation begins with the art of observation. It will be difficult for any secretary to anticipate effectively if she is not a student of human behavior.

Almost without exception, executive secretaries are good observers. For example, a secretary knows by the chemistry in the air when the boss is not in a very good mood and therefore wouldn't be receptive to a discussion of her vacation plans. Conversely, she recognizes when the atmosphere is more positive. This kind of observation is learned. Some secretaries are better at it than others. Some develop an instinct for it, so that they can even spot it from voice tone over the telephone.

Some may question whether anticipation can be learned. By becoming a better observer, you'll find that you'll draw conclusions that will enable you to anticipate certain actions. You hope that the executive does not have wild swings of moods (and he hopes you don't either), but no person is exactly the same every day. To expect complete evenness of mood is not realistic.

There are some situations where anticipation is fairly obvious. If you take a call from someone in St. Louis who wants the executive to call back about the possibility of leasing some space, attaching the St. Louis lease file to the telephone message may seem obvious. The inexperienced secretary who isn't thinking about what she's doing will leave the phone memo without the St. Louis file. In fact, she may not even impart the subject matter of the call, even when she has the information. This moves us into a delicate area.

Some executives with great faith in an experienced secretary will encourage or even ask her to inquire about the subject matter on calls they have to return. Others don't want the secretary to ask. This second group may feel that the person at the other end of the phone may be turned off by a secretary probing into the subject matter. If your boss falls into the second category, take the message and the return number and let it go at that. If you're not sure how your boss feels about it, ask him. However, it's reasonably safe to assume most executives only want an experienced and tactful secretary asking questions about the nature of the call.

Even calls that are about business are considered personal by the person making them. If your boss is willing to have you attempt to secure more information so that he will be better prepared when he returns the call, it's mandatory that you use a large supply of tact and diplomacy. You might try this kind of approach: "Could you tell me the nature of the call, so that I can pull the correct file for Mr. Valentine and not hold you on the phone unnecessarily?"

It's true that many seasoned executives will volunteer the nature of the call when they find the person they want to talk to is not there and will have to return the call. It's also true that no matter how tactful you are, you may get an answer such as: "Oh, he knows what I'm calling about," or "It's a personal matter." If the person at the other end doesn't want to give you any information, don't press the matter.

Another way to anticipate is to look in the pending alphabetical file we discussed in a previous chapter and see if there are any pending files on people who have called and want to have their calls returned. This again is a matter of executive preference. Some executives may prefer to wait and buzz you while they are on the phone if they need the file. Some preparations for meetings could be considered "anticipation," but meetings play such a major role in business life today that a separate chapter will be devoted to them.

Here are other examples of anticipation:

- The executive is having lunch away from the office with another executive. Early in the morning, the secretary could ask her boss if he'd like her to call a restaurant and make a reservation for lunch.
- The executive mentions he's going to take his car into the shop over the lunch hour. The secretary asks if he'd like her to call and make certain the shop can provide him with courtesy transportation back to the office.
- If your company has a practice of meeting executives at the local airport when they return from a business trip, the secretary should notify the person in charge of such ground transportation of the flight number and the arrival time.

Another example of anticipation has to do with the open door that exists in most offices. Very few executives work with their door closed unless they don't want to be disturbed or interrupted. As a result, people have a tendency to walk into an executive's office if the door is open and he is alone. What may start off as an open discussion may develop into a private conversation. If either the executive or the visitor starts raising his voice, the secretary should quietly get up and close the office door.

An employee may be inside the office telling her boss,

"I'm not being paid enough for what I do." She should close the door because what follows will be a confidential conversation about the employee's salary. Occasionally, the executive will beat her to the punch and close the door before a raised voice ever reaches her area.

Most managers leave their doors open because they don't like the isolated feeling that comes from having the door closed and because they can get an idea of what's going on outside their doors.

A seasoned secretary who has worked with the same executive for a long time can tell when he's troubled. Sometimes all that's required to get him over it is a willingness to listen or an offer to help. She might say, "I can tell something's troubling you. Is there anything I can do?" or "Do you want to talk about it?" An executive occasionally needs to have someone to talk to about what's on his mind. He may not be able to talk to his superior about it, because the superior may be part of the problem. He can't talk to his peers about it, because he's competing with them for the next promotion. He may not be able to discuss it with his subordinates, because he's afraid they might misunderstand some of the implications. Perhaps he can't discuss it with his wife, because he'd have to supply too much office background for her to understand the problem. The wife can sometimes function as a listening post, but not always. When she can't, the secretary often can. All the executive may need is someone to listen who is not threatening to him. Confidentiality is a must and we'll talk more about that in a subsequent chapter.

When the executive's desk looks like a disaster area, whether because of work brought with him from a business trip or material he was working on at home, an offer to help is always appreciated. Too many secretaries consider their own work separate from that of their boss. Actually there's a job to do, with two people to get it done, and those two people are the executive and the secretary.

Unfortunately a secretary may get her mind set on doing her filing and resent being called away from it because that's what she has decided to do. Taking care of an emergency that has developed is more important than doing the filing, which has been laying there for three days anyway. Some secretaries consider the work on their desks as their top priority and consequently don't feel free to do other things, even for their boss. The executive sets the priorities for his own position and that of his secretary.

Another way a secretary can practice the art of anticipation is to look at the executive's calendar and see what meetings and appointments he has scheduled for the next week. The secretary should then ask herself what items he is likely to need for these appointments and what she can do to help him prepare for them. The answers to those questions are the practice of the art of anticipation. Early in the secretary's relationship with the executive she might ask him what he will need for those appointments and how she might help. That's a basic way for her to learn how she can be most useful.

It may seem like a "damned if you do, damned if you don't" proposition, but many executives complain because their secretaries will assume nothing and others complain because their secretaries assume too much. The middle ground is where you need to be. Exactly where that is depends on your boss. Either doing nothing until you are told or assuming tasks or responsibilities that are not properly yours can lead to difficulties for both you and your boss.

The art of anticipation will become an almost intuitive skill after a while. It's extremely valuable; practice it.

9

Handling Meetings

As I mentioned in my earlier book, *The First-Time Manager,* I suspect the productivity of the nation could be increased dramatically if all meetings were banned for one year. Unfortunately, such a revolutionary idea will not catch on, so we might as well accept the fact that there will be meetings. Our concern here is to make them productive at best or, failing that, to make them as harmless as possible.

A camel has been described as a horse put together by a committee. Another wag has suggested that meetings or committees were invented as a way of spreading the blame. To that, I would add that they are a way of spreading the blame among so many people that its damage is nothing more than an inconvenience to the participants.

As an executive, your boss is going to be subject to meetings called on the spur of the moment, regular meetings he attends as a member, and committees of which he functions as chairman. There's not a lot you can do about spur-of-the-moment meetings, except to get whatever files or reports your boss may think he needs as he goes dashing out the door. Usually this kind of meeting develops because of an emergency or because someone thinks there might be a problem if action isn't taken.

Aside from emergency meetings, committee gatherings

have a regular meeting date or are "on call" by the chairman. Meeting dates should be put on your boss's desk calendar. Although some people may disagree, I think there is some advantage to noting it on the calendar of the day before also. I am assuming your boss uses a calendar that has a page for each day in the year. I believe it's helpful to note it on the page for the day before the meeting so that when the executive goes home from work, he realizes there is a meeting at eight the next morning. In addition to putting it on the calendar, it is helpful if the secretary reminds him as she leaves the office: "Don't forget, you have a budget committee meeting tomorrow morning at eight o'clock."

Many executives now carry pocket calendars. They have become valuable additions to the "modus operandi" of an executive because of his many activities away from the office. If he's on the board of the YMCA, he needs to know what his schedule looks like when that board is talking about a special planning meeting. Without the pocket calendar he won't know what commitments he's already made.

The executive can be in trouble if you mark a meeting on his desk calendar without making certain it also gets in his pocket calendar. There are several ways to do this. One is to leave a note on his desk suggesting he mark his pocket calendar when you mark a meeting on his desk calendar. Another is to make a note of it and bring it up at the next morning's daily meeting. He'll then mark the pocket calendar.

If the secretary starts to put a meeting on her boss's desk calendar and notices that he is already booked for that particular time, it's essential that she bring the conflict to his attention as soon as possible so that he can resolve it. Often he'll have her call the secretary of the committee's chairman and communicate the fact that he "can't make the meeting because he's going to be in New York on business."

The secretary shouldn't decide which meetings her boss

will or will not attend. If there's a conflict on the calendar, calling it to the attention of the executive is sufficient. He'll decide which meeting he'll go to. You can't always assume the meeting already on the desk calendar is more important than the second meeting called. The first one may consist of rather mundane matters, while the second may have substance to it and be the meeting he chooses to attend. Only the executive should make such a decision. He'll have a better idea of the probable content of the meetings and is in a better position to decide which to attend.

A file should be established for every committee on which the executive sits that meets on a regular basis. The minutes should be filed on the left with all other matters placed on the right side of the file. I know some secretaries prefer to file everything in chronological order on the right side of the file, and then move to the left side when the right half of the file won't hold another piece of paper.

Experience has taught me that the minutes should be placed on one side by themselves. Most of the references made back into the file seem to be related to action or discussion at a previous meeting. As a result, you're more likely to review minutes than any other documents in the file. It's easier to find an item in previous minutes if all the minutes are on one side of the file and you don't have to wade through other, extraneous papers to locate them. With committee meetings that manufacture a lot of paper, you may need to consider a separate file for the minutes, because a new file that has no minutes could be a problem.

Some people consider it unnecessary for a committee member to carry minutes to a meeting. The reason they feel this way is that usually the committee secretary or the chairman has a copy so if anyone needs to look at them, they are available. I disagree. Most of the time the executive wants to look at minutes during a meeting for reasons he wouldn't want to discuss openly, not because there's anything wrong with his inquiry, but because it may not be something to take the whole committee's time. For example, if he hears someone arguing for a position he believes is contrary to the way that person voted when the matter was last considered, he wouldn't want to ask that question openly. But with the ability to look back at the minutes, he can verify or refute his feeling that the other member changed his position. He will then be a more effective committee member. He will be able to say, "George, I'm interested in your argument, because as I recall you didn't always feel that way." There are other reasons he might want to look back at the minutes privately. He might want to see how he voted on a particular issue at a previous meeting. He may want to know when an item was previously discussed.

The use of the minutes often depends on how extensive they are. Very few committees keep full transcripts unless they are legally required to do so. Most committees attempt to capture the highlights of the meetings. Many will show whether or not a motion was carried. Some will carry the vote and some will not. Many companies keep informal minutes. In fact, in some organizations, members feel the secretary must have attended a different meeting, because the minutes bear little relationship to actual events.

Another reason for having the minutes is it helps to avoid unnecessary disagreements and to straighten out faulty memories. Most members will not carry a set of minutes to a meeting, so those who do are better informed.

Nearly every committee chairman prepares an agenda before a meeting. If he's conscientious, he will do it. The question is whether the agenda will be distributed before the meeting or the chairman will keep it a secret. As strange as it may seem, some chairmen don't want committee members to be too well prepared or "loaded for bear," as it were.

A chairman who doesn't feel threatened will have no objection to preparing and distributing an agenda in advance. This will enable the executive to be better prepared when he goes to the meeting. Committee members who have the opportunity to prepare for a meeting are more likely to make a better contribution to the group's deliberations. The better prepared the committee, the more efficiently the committee will function.

The agenda that comes to an executive well in advance of the meeting provides the secretary with the opportunity to help him prepare. This can be the subject of one of the daily meetings. It comes under the heading of items the secretary wishes to discuss.

The secretary can hand the agenda to her boss with these words: "Here's the agenda for next Friday's planning meeting. Are there any items on the agenda that require some advance work? Any files you want me to pull? What do we need to do to prepare for the meeting?"

A discussion of the politics of meetings may now be in order. An understanding of the problems may help the secretary appreciate the necessity for preparation.

No executive wants to look stupid at a meeting. He doesn't want to appear uninformed. Many executives believe that promotions and salary increases are related to the impression they create at meetings. The committee meeting may be one of the few opportunities your boss has to impress executives in the organization who outrank him. He's of the opinion that how he's viewed by these people is important to his career. He may be right. Many promotions are based on a chief executive's impression of an individual. It's not how he looks, although that may be a part of it. It's how he thinks, how he thinks on his feet, how he articulates his views, how logical he appears to be, the depth of his knowledge, and so on.

Even if your boss is beyond the point in his career where he's still after a promotion, no executive wants to look bad at a meeting. Executives usually have large egos, in spite of how hard some of them work at appearing humble. Unfortunately, these egos bruise easily. Looking uninformed at a meeting is a big bruise, and if you are somehow responsible for his lack of preparation you're going to hear about it—in spades.

If your boss is chairman of the committee, there's another whole series of opportunities (sometimes called problems) for you. You will be responsible for agendas, minutes, room reservations, and maybe even the coffee. Let's hope you're working for a secure executive who will be willing to distribute the agenda in advance of the meeting. The timing of these matters is personal and may vary by executive. I think you can send out the agenda too early. A week before the meeting is about right.

Obviously, the reason for distributing the agenda is to give the members of the committee advance notice of the subject matters to be discussed. These committee members then have the opportunity to prepare themselves. Whether they do or not is up to them; at least they had adequate notice. Members of a committee appreciate advance knowledge of the business to be considered.

Along with the agenda, there may be exhibits to be attached. Again, this depends on the attitude of the committee chairman. Company practice may play a part in the decision. If there's a long position paper or a lengthy technical report to be considered, there are many reasons to recommend sending it with the agenda. One of the primary reasons is so that it can be read in advance of the meeting. There's seldom anything more deadly than a committee meeting consisting of a dozen people sitting around a conference table reading a report they could have read at their own pace in the privacy of their offices. Also, if the matter is highly technical, people can't or won't spend the time making certain they understand all facets of the report. If they have questions about the report, some are unlikely to ask for fear of looking dull or slow in front of their associates.

It's possible for a chairman to manipulate a committee by not giving it the clearance to read these technical reports in

advance. The chairman might feel he can get some po
rammed through because members will be reluctan
admit they don't understand the report. This is a danger
game to play. Several executives on the committee coul
have enough confidence in themselves to admit they
haven't had enough time to understand the report
thoroughly. Any chairman who approaches a committee
with the idea of manipulating it is headed for trouble.

The secretary should send the agenda to the members of
the committee in a sealed envelope. Putting an agenda
through the company's routing system with only a routing
tag makes the agenda public information. There may not
necessarily be anything confidential on the agenda, but the
committee members deserve the courtesy of the knowledge
before everyone else has it. Anyone who believes this is a
minor point doesn't realize the effectiveness of the
grapevine in an organzation. To prove the point I can relate
a personal experience.

Before our company moved to our present location a
number of years ago, we occupied a five-story building. To
test the effectiveness of our grapevine, I took the elevator
to the fifth floor. After my charade of being there on business, I made up a rumor, which I told to a person I suspected was a key person in the company's grapevine. I then
walked the stairs back to my desk on the first floor. As I sat
down, the young man at the next desk leaned over and
asked me if I'd heard the latest. He then repeated the rumor
I'd just manufactured on the fifth floor.

Total time elapsed to travel five floors was 12¾ minutes.
From that point in my business career, I've never under-
estimated the speed and efficiency of the grapevine. By
routing agendas openly you may be putting items in the
grapevine that don't belong there. Play it safe and put all
premeeting material in sealed envelopes. The members of
the committee will appreciate it.

If the meeting takes place on a regular schedule, there's

usually no problem with the meeting room. You can secure it on a permanent basis if your organization reserves meeting rooms. If the committee meets on an irregular basis, you must make sure a meeting place is reserved. If the meeting is going to take place at a different location than is customary or at an unusual time for the committee, there is a temptation to make such information the lead sentence on the agenda. Although you have taken care of your responsibility with such an approach, it's not the most effective way of communicating.

Executives are not alone in missing obvious information. Many people are guilty of this failing. The first line of the agenda can give the meeting place and the time and some of the members will never see it. They'll go to the place the committee usually meets and at the usual time. They assume in glancing at the agenda that the first line says what it always says and go straight to the meat of the transmittal, which is the meeting agenda itself. You are correct in thinking people shouldn't scan over important, fundamental items, but they do. Your objective is to get them to the right place at the right time.

A separate strip of paper of a different color should be stapled to the agenda with words such as, "Please note a change in time and meeting room. The meeting will be at 8:30 A.M. in the third floor west conference room." Anyone who then gets the time or place wrong will hardly qualify as a "quick study."

The organization's practice or tradition will determine whether coffee is served at the meetings. In some companies, coffee is served only if it's an early morning meeting. In others, coffee is never served. Still others fall somewhere between these two extremes.

Let's make a couple of assumptions. Let's assume it's an early morning meeting, coffee is traditional, and the secretary doesn't stay for the entire meeting. If the meeting begins at 8:30, the secretary ought to have the coffee and all the other necessary accouterments there by 8:25. Several different methods can be used. Any of them is acceptable, depending on the preference of the chairman of the committee.

1. As the members enter the meeting room, the secretary can ask them if they'd like a cup of coffee. If a member says yes, the secretary fills a coffee cup and hands it to him. The committee member then takes care of his or her own cream or sugar.
2. The coffee can already be poured. As people walk in, they simply pick up a cup and take their place at the table. The cream and sugar are on the table and they help themselves.
3. The people come in and take their seats. The secretary asks them if they'd like a cup of coffee and serves it to them.
4. The secretary puts the coffee and all the accouterments in the room, leaves, and allows everyone to serve himself as he enters the room.

These various methods will all get the job done, although I consider the fourth method the least satisfactory. It lacks the personal touch that exists in the other three. Many people think such shading is unimportant, but these little nuances make a difference in people's reactions. Method 4 is cold and impersonal. The other three have a personal touch that makes people feel important. If the secretary has a hang-up about serving people, she might prefer method 4 because she could get the material there and get out.

Not everyone drinks coffee. If some members of the committee would prefer hot tea, iced tea, or decaffeinated coffee, by all means have it available for them. You can find out what they want at the first meeting. However, if a new committee is about to have its first meeting, there's a simple way to find out what the members drink. Call their secretaries and ask them what their bosses prefer. The committee members attending that first meeting will be impressed, especially if the secretary is able to say as Mr. Johnson walks into the meeting, "We have decaffeinated coffee for you, Mr. Johnson." The secretary who pays attention to such nice little touches will soon get the reputation of being a "class executive secretary." Often the difference between an executive secretary who is considered "class" and one who is considered "ordinary" is attention to subtle nuances and attitude.

When you serve the coffee, be guided by how the executive you're working for prefers it to be done. If he wants you to bring the coffee, leave it, and run, by all means do it that way. If he has no preference, use a method with a more personal touch. The other executives will tell him, sooner or later, how lucky he is to have such a thoughtful secretary. A thoughtful secretary—one with all the other skills, of course—may find herself promoted to secretary of the chief executive. The difference between the person who has the best secretarial position in the organization and all the others often is a sensitivity to people and attention to detail. Little things can mean a lot.

There still may be companies in which the secretary of the committee chairman takes the minutes of the meeting. This is a heavy responsibility if it must be done exclusively with shorthand. Many organizations, especially government or other public bodies, have augmented this shorthand by tape recording the entire process. When the entire meeting is tape recorded, the secretary can use the tape to clear up any doubtful items in her notes. Other organizations have someone transcribe the entire proceedings in rough draft form and then capture the highlights from the draft. This puts a heavy responsibility on the secretary. I consider it an unfair burden for her.

If you are required to condense the minutes from a transcript, be sure that all votes are covered in the minutes. It's a good idea to have the chairman of the committee review the minutes and see if he believes you've succeeded in capturing the important business that was transacted.

Although you may never have to refer to it again, take the entire verbatim transcript to the next meeting, just in case a discussion occurs related to the previous meeting. I think it's also important to save the tapes from the meetings. Perhaps they only need to be saved for a specified period— say, one year. The thought is that if no one objects in twelve months, objections are unlikely. You could recycle the tapes by using one that is thirteen months old each month.

Condensing transcripts down to satisfactory minutes is not easy. Many executives don't realize how difficult it is. What makes it particularly vexing is that in an effort to capture everything, you don't have the luxury of sitting there, leaning back in your chair to assimilate all the conversation, and then understanding the bigger concept that is evolving. Transcribing every word is recording all the trees; as a result you may not be able to realize the depth of the forest.

The primary responsibility for satisfactory minutes lies with the chairman of the committee, not the secretary. Therefore, the secretary should have the executive review the draft of the minutes before they're distributed.

I feel that better minutes can be taken if the secretary doesn't attempt to transcribe every word, but is allowed to sit back and drink in the concept or the bigger meaning before attempting to summarize it. This may be one reason more committees are not using secretaries to take the minutes, but are selecting one of the voting members to capture the highlights. Such a member should be more familiar with the concepts being discussed. There are strong arguments on both sides of the question. It may depend on how formal the committee must be. If it's a committee required by law or a public body, an actual word-by-word transcript may be necessary. In most companies the committee is an informal device, and the minutes are not critical.

I have been on committees where I looked at the minutes and was convinced that the recorder had in fact attended some other meeting. Whether you're taking a transcript or attempting to capture the highlights, try to make them as accurate as you can.

10

Indispensability

Most people want to become indispensable to their boss and to their company or organization. At the same time, most people also want to rise in the organization. The two attitudes are in conflict with one another. If you become indispensable, your chances of being promoted are greatly diminished.

Let's take care of what may be a myth many executives perpetuate. They pay lip service to the concept that they don't mind if their secretaries are promoted. Many of them mind a great deal; some would actually stand in the way of the secretary getting a promotion. Some won't stand in the way, but won't do much to help either. That's telling it like it is.

These attitudes create a problem for the executive secretary who does want a promotion. The secretary's own attitude also plays a role. The secretary may want to be indispensable as job security. She may believe (and I'll admit it happens now and then) that if she makes it easier for the executive to function without her, she'll be more subject to losing her job, if he should get upset some day.

For many secretaries, the sweetest words they can hear when they return from a vacation are: "Thank God you're back. I had a terrible time finding anything while you were gone." One reason her boss may have had trouble is because she hid things. The fault in such a situation lies with the executive who has allowed the secretary to structure the job in a way that permitted such foolishness. However, some executives unwittingly encourage a secretary to become indispensable. They make such statements as, "I don't care how you maintain the files, as long as you can find what I want," or, "I don't care about the details of your job."

At some point an executive has to have an interest in how the secretary's job is structured. It should happen when he first comes into the job. He should be involved in deciding how the files are to be maintained, how the mail is to be processed, how the advance file system operates, and how all the important facets of the secretary's position will be carried out. If he doesn't know enough and isn't able to explain the general concept to a new secretary, he runs the risk of having every new secretary restructure the job to her own liking. The result may be utter chaos when one of them leaves unexpectedly. He may find a bizarre filing system like the one my friend and I found in the district office described previously. If an executive doesn't let a secretary know what he wants, he has no one to blame but himself if she puts together a system that makes no sense to anyone but her.

I don't mean to imply that an executive has to sit with a secretary and show her what to do step by step. That's unnecessary if she's worked as a secretary before. However, he should be able to explain the concept of what he wants.

Even if a secretary figures this job is the zenith and she has no higher aspirations in the organization, the executive still shouldn't allow her to make herself indispensable. It's not in her best interest, either. If she succeeds in making the executive helpless without her, he'll never want her to take a full three-week vacation at one time. About the most she can ever hope for is one week, and he'd prefer that she not take more than two or three days at once.

If you're home in bed with the flu and running a 103°

temperature, he'll call you. When you're ready to sit down at the table for a nice quiet candlelight dinner, he'll call asking about some file. On a Saturday morning, as you're about to go out the door, heading for a weekend at the beach, he'll call and insist you come into the office; an emergency has arisen and he needs you. If you're thinking of becoming indispensable, consider the price you may have to pay. Being indispensable isn't all it's cracked up to be.

The enlightened executive will resent a secretary who attempts to make herself indispensable, because it makes him dependent. If you move in that direction you may find yourself in some difficulty.

There are executives, however, who permit a secretary to become indispensable because they themselves are inadequate. That may happen in spite of the efforts of a secretary to prevent it. Those with decided shortcomings easily become dependent upon any talented secretary who works for them.

A secretary can use several techniques to avoid or at least minimize the indispensability problem. One method is to prepare a desk manual that shows all the major functions of the job. It's best to use a three-ring looseleaf folder with a separate page for each task.

Give the task a simple title and follow it with a simple statement of the objective, unless it's so obvious that a restatement would be redundant. "Open the mail" would be an example of an obvious task. Next, outline the steps you have to take to do the job. If there are any steps you follow to recheck yourself, be sure to list them too. Start with what you consider the major parts of the job and keep going until you've listed every important duty. This is the kind of project you might work on for months before it's complete. I'd suggest you put each page in a plastic cover.

You will reap an added advantage in taking on such a project. As you review these tasks, you may find that you're taking some unnecessary steps. As a result you'll be able to streamline some of the functions of your job. You'll achieve a far better understanding of your duties as an executive secretary by working through this project.

As you make pages, make a photocopy of each page and take it home. Maintain a duplicate copy of the desk manual at home. You may never use it. On the other hand, a time may come when you're home on vacation or ill and your boss or a co-worker wants to discuss a certain procedure with you. It's easier to do if you're both looking at the same write-up rather than if you have the other person read parts of it to you over the telephone.

Another useful approach in avoiding the indispensability problem is to cross-train. Strange as it may seem, the physical layout of the office has an effect on cross-training. If you're working outside a senior executive's office in an isolated section of the building, cross-training is more difficult because someone has to leave her work area to come to your desk for cross-training sessions. In many companies executive offices are clustered together and executive secretaries share a combination work/reception area. Cross-training is easier under such circumstances.

The first rule to follow in cross-training is to talk to your boss about it. He may have a preference as to what aspects of the job are covered by the cross-training. He will probably want to visit with his associate to make certain they are in agreement about it. Remember that when you're training the other secretary to be able to do your job you will be learning her responsibilities.

Another reason you need to talk to your boss before such an undertaking is to see if there are any areas of his work and therefore your work that he considers too confidential for you to share with someone else's secretary.

You have a responsibility not to recommend cross-training with the office gossip. Your boss may not know what she is, but if you know she gossips, you have a responsibility to tell him before he agrees to the cross-training. He would never agree if he had any inkling his work was going to be exposed to the company grapevine. Don't assume you can tell this secretary something's confidential and she'll respect your request. You must assume that she'll spill the beans.

There may be other reasons your boss will not agree to cross-training with another executive's secretary. It may depend on his relationship with his counterpart. They may be competitors for a promotion or a committee chairmanship they both consider crucial to their career advancement. He may want to select another executive that he doesn't consider a threat. Office politics may enter into his decision as to which secretary he wants cross-training with his secretary.

Cross-training is a two-way street. If the other secretary is going to learn your job, it follows that you'll have to be trained in her position, too. If not, there's nothing in it for the other executive and his secretary. Most cross-training is done to cover vacations, sick days, and unexpected absences. It follows that when you cover someone else's desk plus your own, you can't do both jobs as completely as when two secretaries are on the job.

Both your boss and the absent secretary's boss understand you can't cover both positions completely. Your duties need to be defined by you and your boss after the cross-training is completed. Ideally, the discussion should take place among both executives and both secretaries. However, you might have to start by having a discussion with your own boss. Then, perhaps, you could suggest a meeting of the foursome. He may not go for it. He may make a counterproposal, that he and his executive counterpart discuss the matter.

The conversation you have might cover some of the following options:

1. "When his secretary is gone, do you want me covering most of our work and doing only his emergency work?"

2. "I could try to cover the major functions of both jobs, like opening the mail, pulling files for the incoming mail, and trying to take care of the necessary dictation for both of you."

3. "Some tasks for both of you will have to wait. For example, I doubt that I can keep up with the filing."

4. "Do you expect me to take care of his meetings, agendas, coffee, and so on?"

The kind of work on which you cross-train will generate other items of discussion, but the above examples give you an idea of the problems that are possible and probable.

Filling in for a secretary who is on vacation is one of the most frustrating tasks of executive secretaries. The executive's workload doesn't slow down because his secretary is on vacation. Like the Mississippi River it just keeps rolling along, and although executives may agree that a secretary couldn't possibly cover both desks, sometimes they get upset if their own work is not kept up. In such situations, an executive secretary may have to take the executive back to the previous conversation and remind him what the agreement was.

It's possible that neither executive will be satisfied with the level of work you can do while the other executive's secretary is on vacation. It may be satisfactory for the occasional day off, but not for longer periods. Some companies use temporary help from outside the office or have a pool of people in the company who can fill in. However, many executives will still look to you as the executive secretary to take care of items with which temporary help (either outside or inside) can't possibly be familiar.

The best you can hope for if you have to cover both desks is to prevent any major fires from erupting. It's obvious that if you can handle the work of both desks, one of you is not needed.

In some companies, one secretary takes care of the work

of two executives. The workload requiring executive secretary assistance varies a great deal not only between companies but even within the same organization. I have known of two high-level executives who got by very well sharing a secretary while at a lower level, a middle manager's workload and responsibilities required the assistance of a full-time secretary.

The desk manual is useful when someone is filling in on your job. Also, if you're filling in on another desk you'll get first-hand experience of its value as part of the cross-training process.

In an effort to minimize the problems of cross-training, some executives insist that their secretaries take their vacations when they do. This probably adds to the indispensability problem, because it assumes the secretary will be out only when she's on vacation. In fact, a prolonged illness can create the identical problem, so having the secretary take her vacation at the same time doesn't solve the problem.

Some companies close and have the entire workforce take its vacation at one time. This won't work for most organizations, and only diminishes the need for cross-training. It adds to the problem of indispensability. The secretary may see no need for a desk manual or for cross-training. When an illness or accident occurs, the problem is intensified.

It's difficult for many secretaries to convince themselves that they should avoid indispensability. It may be contrary to their survival instinct. However, I hope I have convinced the readers of this book that it is in their best interest.

11

Confidentiality and the Confidence Crisis

If you were to ask 100 secretaries if confidentiality was important in their work, ninety-nine of them would say, "Of course," but most of the ninety-nine would be guilty of violating confidentiality on a regular basis. They would not do it intentionally, but the impact of the violation would be just as damaging.

Confidentiality is important in two areas: in how the work is processed and in the attitude of the secretary and oral communication. One cardinal rule for an executive secretary to follow is, "If you don't know for certain, assume it's confidential." You may think me guilty of overkill on the question of keeping confidences, but your boss would rather you erred on the cautious than on the loose side.

When you come out of your boss's office after taking dictation, don't allow your shorthand pad to lie on top of your desk while you go on your coffee break or leave the area for any other reason. There are people who will come by, stand there, and read your shorthand. If you're not going to transcribe your notes right away, put them in your desk, where they won't be a temptation for anyone. The same is true of a partially typed letter in your typewriter. Don't leave it there for someone to stand and read while you're gone.

Do you save your shorthand after the letter has been

signed? Why? Tear it up and throw it away. If you can't bear to destroy the pad, keep it in a file that's locked after office hours.

Lock your files and your desk at night. If your boss is out of the office, make certain his desk and files are locked before you leave.

Do you route interoffice letters in the mail system without putting them in envelopes? You might as well post them on the bulletin board. Always put interoffice letters in envelopes, and if only the person being addressed should be reading the contents, mark the envelopes "personal and confidential." Some executives have their secretaries open all their mail, even if it is marked "personal and confidential." That's something you can't control. But if, as you're typing the letter, you believe it is the kind of message your boss wouldn't want his counterpart's secretary reading, you should bring it to his attention. He may not realize the other secretary opens *all* the mail. Some people have gone to a stronger warning on the envelope, marking it "to be opened by addressee only."

When you tell your boss the other secretary opens all his mail, you may be asked to deliver the envelope personally to the executive addressed. When you get to his office you may find he's not in, and his secretary will tell you to leave it. If you've been told to hand-deliver it to the addressee, don't leave it with his secretary. Report back to your boss that you couldn't deliver it. He may then call the other executive's office and ask for the call to be returned. When it's returned, he can say, "I've got a confidential message. I want my secretary to hand to you personally. She'll be right over."

An executive secretary is constantly exposed to confidental material. It can become so matter of fact the secretary may lose sight of the sensitive nature of the information.

Coffee-break gossip can create havoc, especially if the

secretary is prone to discuss items that shouldn't be made known to others. There are people who consider it a challenge to draw confidential information out of people. They can be clever about the way they do it. Sometimes the approach is to imply that the executive secretary isn't in on what's going on in the company, that her boss keeps confidential or *really* important matters from her. The scheme is to get the secretary to prove the accuser wrong by sharing some highly confidential matter with the others. This approach is so childish I wouldn't think any executive secretary would fall for it.

I can think of few things more damaging to the working relationship between an executive and his secretary than for the secretary to violate a confidence. Once it happens, the executive will never completely trust the secretary again. It's similar to discovering a close friend has stolen something of value from you. No matter how remorseful the friend is, and even if the straight-and-narrow path is trod from that point on, the trust that was there originally can never be restored completely. You can glue the handle back on the cup, but the crack is still there.

A secretary is tempted to have and perhaps even needs a confidant in the office. This is understandable. Everyone needs someone to whom he can talk. A secretary can't depend exclusively on the executive with whom she works for confidential conversations. You need a friend who'll listen, understand, and still be your friend. The need for this kind of relationship exists in nearly all of us.

One idea that may work is to develop this kind of relationship with another executive secretary who has the same kind of responsibility. This person will understand the confidential nature of the job, and will often be privy to the same information. You will each have an opportunity to discuss your work without violating confidences. Of course, there will still be things you shouldn't discuss, even with your confidant. For example, if your boss makes an uncomplimentary remark about his mother-in-law or his wife, it shouldn't be repeated. He may express some disappointment in a teenage son or daughter. Don't mention it.

There may be times when the secretary discusses her personal problems with the executive. She wouldn't want the executive to tell his associates what she said while he's lunching in the executive dining room. She should apply the same standards to him that she expects him to uphold to her.

It's a mistake to share a confidence with a friend at the office and then tell him or her that it's confidential and must not be repeated. Unfortunately, some people use confidential information as an ego booster. They can't wait to go to a friend or acquaintance and say, "I've got something you must promise not to repeat." It's usually all over the office before the day is out.

You must analyze your own motivation. Does it make you feel important to be able to tell somebody something he's not likely to have heard before? It does make most of us feel important, but the degree may be significant. An executive secretary must resist the temptation to bolster her own self-importance this way.

I was once affiliated with an organization that required a group to travel together extensively. Boredom often set in. One person was the self-appointed vice-president in charge of rumors. His task was to start rumors that were untrue but plausible. Occasionally he'd toss something in that was true to keep everybody off balance. It relieved the boredom, because he was both inventive and creative. I'm not suggesting that an executive secretary should start rumors, but if you have to have your ego bolstered, it might be preferable to violating confidences. Perhaps you can let people in on secrets that have nothing to do with the office.

Salaries are usually a confidential matter in most organizatons. The exception is for government jobs, where salaries are a matter of public record. In private enterprise, however, they are seldom discussed. The secretary's salary is between the company, the executive, and herself. The same is true of salary increases and their frequency.

There is much misunderstanding about why many companies keep salary information confidential. Uninformed people believe it's so companies can pay more money to top executives and to favorite employees without having to justify their actions. I'll even admit that sometimes that's true. But the main reason companies keep salary information confidential is so they can pay more for outstanding performance than for mediocre work.

When salary information is a matter of public record, there is a tendency to pay everyone at the same level approximately the same salary, the major variation being seniority on the job. Neither job level nor time on the job is of itself a good reason for paying someone more money. You ought to pay more money to the people who are doing the best job for the organization.

In spite of performance appraisals and attempts to make them as objective as possible, it's impossible to eliminate subjectivity completely. If salary information is confidential you can pay the outstanding performers more without having to go through a big hassle with all the people who think they're better than management thinks they are.

You may have some personal feelings about whether salary information should be confidential or general information. A case can be made for the argument that if a company can't defend its salary increases, it doesn't have a very good program. However, when we talk about what someone is worth, we find that none of us can be objective about ourselves. I have never known a talented executive or executive secretary who thought he or she was overpaid. Most talented people believe that their salaries never catch up with their performance. Many people who are not so talented also feel that way; that's where the problem starts.

Most of us rationalize our performance on the job. We

convince ourselves that the tasks we perform well are the crucial ones and that those we do less well aren't as important. Therefore, since the things that are crucial are performed so admirably, we obviously are underpaid. We really are worth more money; others just think they are.

People may try to draw you out about your salary or about a salary increase. Since most companies have a formal salary administration program, usually everyone knows when salary increases go through. Some may even be so bold as to volunteer what they are paid for the specific purpose of getting you to disclose your own salary.

Here are some lines you may find helpful when someone attempts to draw you into a salary discussion:

If someone starts to discuss his or her salary, you can usually stop that person by saying, "I'd really rather not know what anyone else is being paid. Then I don't have to think about whether they're overpaid or underpaid."

Should someone try to discover what you received in the way of a salary increase, you might try this line, "I was pleased with it, although I guess one always wishes it were more."

Here's a more direct response: "I was told by my boss that salaries are a matter of confidentiality around here, and he expects me to honor that. So, as much as I'd enjoy it, I'm afraid I'll have to pass on this discussion."

Sometimes a more frivolous answer about your salary or your raise will get the message across: "I'm getting a lot less than I think I'm worth, and probably more than you think I'm worth."

Here's an answer I've used on the subject of finances in general that usually turns the conversation away from me: "If I had half as much money as people think I have, I'd have twice as much as I've got."

Many executive secretaries are asked to process their boss's check if he is out of the office on payday. If your boss asks you to do this for him, it's the ultimate compliment. It means he trusts you and has no qualms about your knowing what his annual salary is. He knows that the first time you process the check, you will probably calculate what he makes a year. He is not uncomfortable with you having that information. If the nature of your work doesn't normally give you access to salary information, including his, you know you've arrived as far as his trust is concerned when he allows you to process his paycheck.

If your company deposits paychecks directly to employees' checking accounts, you may never be asked to process your boss's check. In that case, you'll have to figure out how much he trusts you from other clues. Needless to say, you must guard any confidential information about his personal finances as though you were a member of the C.I.A.

If your boss is a department head or for any other reason manages a large group of people, he is involved in a great number of personnel matters. As part of your work you may have access to the salaries, performance appraisals, personnel applications, attendance records, salary ranges, and perhaps even some of the personal problems employees bring to your boss. He can't survive if these people don't have confidence in him. They won't have confidence in him if they don't also have a great deal of confidence in you as his secretary. They won't tell him what's on their minds if it's a known fact that you have a loose tongue. You'll be making his job much more difficult when it's your responsibility to make his job easier.

You have to develop the confidence of all the people who report to him. Naturally, you're not going to like them all equally. There may be some you can't stand. Still, you must treat them all with respect and respect their confidences. Many will consider you an intermediary with the executive. Some will even try to ingratiate themselves with you with the idea that it's better to have the boss's secretary for them than against. It is important that you treat them all equally.

The person you find the most charming may not be the best performer. For you to sponsor someone because you like him or her can be a mistake, especially if your knowledge of how well that person performs on the job is based on feeling or hearsay. You must maintain credibility with everybody, not just people you like. Without credibility, you will not have the confidence of those in the department. And without confidence, they will filter what they tell you and you won't get the whole story. They will be especially guarded if they feel you're playing favorites among the people in the department.

When your boss seeks your opinion about someone in the department, try to take into consideration the limit of your knowledge of the person. "I don't know what kind of job Joe does in his section, but I've always found him to be pleasant and cooperative. I've never heard anyone say anything derogatory about Joe." Always keep your remarks within the confines of what you know. Don't assume that because someone is very pleasant to you, he's the same way to everyone else. He may very well be, but it's possible that because you're the boss's secretary, you're seeing only someone's best face. You shouldn't look for ulterior motives in everything other people do, but you shouldn't discount them, either.

This subject of confidence and confidentiality is to a large measure a matter of attitude—your own attitude. If you take a flip attitude toward your responsibilities, you probably won't be very concerned about confidentiality.

Years ago, a theological phrase was popular that's not heard much any more. It was called "the seal of the confessional." The concept was that any sin you confessed to your father confessor was so confidential that the clergyman would accept death before he'd reveal anything you'd said to him in the privacy of the confessional. No one would suggest such an extreme standard for an office today. Nevertheless, the importance of confidentiality can't be overemphasized. Your company can be involved in some delicate business matters or negotiations, and the wrong thing leaked to the wrong person could have an adverse effect on the result.

Years ago, executive secretaries were sometimes referred to as confidential secretaries. It's a shame that title fell out of popular usage, because it's an accurate description of the job. You are, in fact, a confidential executive secretary.

12

Personal and Company Loyalty

It's no accident that the chapter on loyalty follows the one on confidentiality. Both character traits are essential to a top-notch executive secretary.

Some people believe that an executive must earn the loyalty of his secretary. I can't quarrel with the statement as a principle; however, before it's earned, a secretary must assume it will be earned. She must start off her first day on the job with the idea that she's going to be loyal to this executive.

Before you conclude that I am suggesting loyalty flows only in one direction, let me hasten to add that the executive must be loyal to the secretary, too. The secretary must also earn this loyalty, but the executive should begin the relationship with the assumption that the loyalty is deserved and warranted.

Unfortunately, loyalty in business is not a popular trait today. It's not in vogue. We are seeing increasing tendencies for people to feel a loyalty to their own professions or even professional associations or groups, but not to the executives or companies that sign their paychecks. We won't dwell on them in great detail, but we might make some assumptions on how the current attitudes developed. I'm sure they didn't come from a single cause.

Periods of relatively high employment of people with professional skills may have been a factor. Competition has been high for quality people. Recruiting doesn't stop in the university placement offices. People are recruited a second, third, and sometimes a fourth time. Keeping a job hasn't been important to people because there have been more jobs than people to fill them. If something suitable didn't open up for people with professional skills as soon as they thought it should, they simply moved on to a company offering the promotion they felt they deserved. An oversupply of such professionals coming out of the nation's colleges and universities ultimately slows down these corporate job jumpers.

Another reason loyalty has not been in vogue has been the attitude of numerous companies. In many cases, people who have moved around among several companies are considered better executive material than those who never left the company. Sometimes those who have stuck with one company have been viewed as lacking in courage by being unwilling to advance their careers by moving around. Without getting into a debate about whether it's best to promote from within or occasionally to bring in some so-called fresh blood from the outside, the fact remains that you can understand why people who have stayed with the company would believe their loyalty was misplaced. This has been going on ever since businesses were first created, but in the past three decades, as the nation has become more and more mobile, it seems to have been increasing.

(I have a theory—completely unproven—about why more and more executive positions are being filled from the outside rather than from within. It's because you know the shortcomings of the people already with you, but not those of the person coming in. He has them, but since you don't know what they are, they're not a factor in the decision. When the shortcomings are discovered, it's too late. In order to avoid having the decision look like a bad one, the company then shores up around the shortcomings and convinces itself that a sound management decision was made.)

The tendency of companies to bring people in from the outside has hurt loyalty to the organization. Another factor has been the increasing tendency toward mergers and acquisitions. People have been burned. They've been loyal to the owners of a company only to have the new owner sell them off. It's not unlike transferring a piece of chattel property or selling a baseball team to the highest bidder.

A person who goes to work for one company is not committed to staying with that organization for the rest of his life. While you're with a company, however, it deserves your loyalty until such time as it proves itself unworthy of it. But you shouldn't assume that either the company or the executive will do something to prove unworthy of your loyalty. That's why I say that loyalty is not unilateral. It works both ways.

Loyalty is a worthwhile trait. A person can't withhold it because of a concern that someday it won't be recognized or appreciated. That would be like not being honest because of the risk that someday someone might cheat you. Good human characteristics are often their own reward.

What is involved in being loyal to your boss? You don't knock him to your associates. You are not two-faced in your relationship with him. You are not all sweetness and light to his face and then stick pins in him when you discuss him with your office friends. Sometimes you are put to the test. You may have an occasional rough day with the boss. However, remember you have bad days, too, and want him to overlook such rare occasions.

There is a temptation to tell all when you've had a disagreement with your boss. If you blast him with your friends at the coffee break, you may not be able to repair the damage tomorrow, when you're no longer upset with him. It's similar to a newspaper printing a retraction of an incorrect story. The people who read the original story seldom see the retraction. You simply can't take back unpleasant things you say. An unpleasant statement is not offset by a compliment. The result of the unpleasant statement may linger longer, especially if you were emotional at the time you made it. Complimentary remarks are seldom made with the same intensity as criticism.

There's another danger. Your friends may not respect your complaint. They may tell others. They may repeat it to their own bosses, who in turn may tell your boss, "I hear through the grapevine that your secretary has been bad-mouthing you." The loyalty among executives to each other, especially when it relates to their secretarial employees, is pretty solid. They may be competitive, but they will report such secretarial indiscretions to the executive involved.

This loyalty extends beyond the office. You don't bad-mouth your boss away from the office either. If you get upset with him occasionally and you must get it out of your system, use the confidant we discussed in a previous chapter. If you can't be loyal to an executive, you shouldn't work for him. This isn't the type of situation you discover after you've been working for him for five years. You'll know in the first few months whether or not this is a person you can respect and to whom you can be loyal. If you can't, by all means look for a different position.

Let's say you're working for someone who has different standards from yours. Everything at the office is satisfactory as far as the work is concerned, but your boss is having an affair with someone. Since you like his wife a great deal, this arrangement upsets you. Unless its impacting upon you and your job, you must stay out of it. As disagreeable as you may find it, what he does away from the office is none of your business, just as what you do away from the office is none of his concern.

If he attempts to drag you into it by expecting you to cover for him or lie to his wife, the situation is different. He has no right to put you in that position and you're perfectly within your rights to tell him you cannot do it. He should respect you for it. If he doesn't, he doesn't deserve you as his secretary.

You may recall the movie *The Apartment*. One of the principal characters, played by Fred MacMurray, fires his secretary, and she retaliates by telling his wife about the affair he is having. The trouble with that kind of an act is that it hurts the innocent party along with the intended victim.

Loyalty to the company should never conflict with loyalty to the executive. They ought to be completely compatible. If they're not, there is a serious problem. You learn a great deal about a person's character when you ask him where he works. If he gives you the name of the firm in an apologetic manner, you get a strong clue about his loyalty. There are people who work only for the paycheck and feel absolutely no loyalty to anyone, but they are not professionals. An executive secretary is a professional.

I don't want to suggest that all organizations deserve your loyalty. Some don't deserve anyone's loyalty. I'm assuming you wouldn't go to work for such a company. It's possible that a company or two in your community exploits its employees and takes advantage of its customers, or operates barely within the law. Unless you're a newcomer to town, you'll know which outfits are questionable. You simply don't go to work for them. If you are new in town, any reputable employment placement office will know the reputation of the firms looking for employees.

Unless you've gone to work for one of these few questionable companies, you should give the organization the benefit of the doubt and assume it deserves your loyalty until proved otherwise. In other words, be trusting, but not naive.

Loyalty to a company means you don't bad-mouth it in the community. You support it and you say positive things about it whenever the opportunity presents itself. This doesn't mean you become a Priscilla Goodshoes and make gushy statements about your company that no one will believe. You can help make your company a better place to work with your own attitude. If you believe that your company has great people working for it, saying so will help spread the word. As the word spreads, the company achieves such a reputation. Other great people are attracted to it, and there is a constant upgrading of the quality of the staff.

Being loyal doesn't mean you close your eyes to the problems existing within the company. Every organization employing human beings has problems. But you don't wash the dirty linen in public. You don't discuss the company's problems outside the company. If someone says to you, "I hear your company is having some problems in the accounting department. What's going on?" your answer might be, if you know there are problems, "That may be. I'm not in that department. Any company of any size has problems. I'm sure it's nothing we can't handle. We're a fine company with great people."

Many people have trouble with loyalty because of their own attitudes. They somehow feel that an employer is someone who can't be trusted and will take unfair advantage of employees at every opportunity. These people have what I referred to in *The First-Time Manager* as the "we and they syndrome." They believe that the company is the mysterious "they" who makes all the rules and keeps the employees ("we") from doing all the things "we" would like to do.

These people feel they must bargain constantly, because "they" are not going to pay one cent more than they must to get the job done. Admittedly, some companies are like that, and they usually get unionized rather quickly. But not all organizations are that way. Some actually want to be above the competition so they can attract and hold better employees. Many companies conduct salary surveys, and know what other companies doing similar work are paying for comparable performance. Most companies want to pay better-than-average salaries for better-than-average performance. The problems arise when people are not willing to perform at better-than-average levels, but want top-of-the-grade compensation.

If the company you work for has a job evaluation system, complete with job descriptions and performance appraisals, it is showing a desire to give better-than-average pay for outstanding performance. Every job evaluation and performance appraisal system is subject to human fallibility, but when a company has such a system you have to give it credit for moving in the right direction, because it is attempting to formulate a system to provide equity. Any company concerned with equity deserves your loyalty until it proves otherwise.

We touched briefly on the possibility of conflict between loyalty to the boss and loyalty to the company, but a few more words are appropriate. There shouldn't be a conflict between the two. The executive secretary is employed by the company to work for the executive. Helping him do his job and look good should not be in conflict with what is in the best interest of the company.

If your boss is dishonest and is stealing from the company, loyalty to that activity is ridiculous. No person of integrity would close her eyes to such traits. But the overwhelming number of executives are honest and talented people. Otherwise, in all probability they wouldn't have risen to their current position on the organization chart.

Loyalty should be given gladly. You'll seldom find it written in a job description, but it's one of the most indispensable tools a secretary can bring to the position.

13

Who the Hell
Is Running This Place?

One of the more sensitive areas to which a secretary has to pay attention is the power of her boss's office. When she requests an item from the supply department, it will get more attention than a requisition from one of the clerks in the mail room. The authority of the executive appears to spread to his secretary. People in the organization will pay a great deal of attention to the secretary of the chief executive officer. As a matter of fact, she may be treated more delicately than other executives in the organization.

It isn't difficult to understand why a secretary would get used to such treatment and soon begin to think it's coming to her because of some special qualities she has or because of the magnetism of her personality. If she doesn't keep such treatment in its proper perspective, she may begin using authority she doesn't really have. The authority of the executive is not automatically transferable to his secretary.

Too many secretaries believe they have the same authority as their boss. As a matter of fact, they do act as an agent for the executive in a limited number of functions. Most of the apparent authority comes from people around the office who want to be perceived positively by the executive and therefore include his secretary in special treatment. Why?

Because she has easier and more frequent access to him than any other person in the office.

It is not unusual for a secretary to have a great working relationship with the executive, a positive perception in the eyes of her fellow secretaries, and an absolutely horrid reputation among the lower-level clerks, the messengers, and the people in the mail room and the supply department. The people in lower-level positions in the company know she's using her boss's authority, which she herself doesn't possess. However, because of her boss, they feel they can't openly respond the way they'd like to, so they say nothing to her face and call her names behind her back.

This type of problem can be avoided with a little tact and diplomacy. Everyone in the office knows this secretary works for an important executive in the company. She doesn't need to give orders. "Mr. Smith must have this by 2:00 o'clock today. I'll be down to get it at 1:30 so I have time to check it out to make sure you've done it right." Such a statement makes enemies because the secretary is throwing her weight around. She can ask and get the same results.

The following approach might be better received: "I'm sorry, but Mr. Smith said he'd need this by 2:00 today. I'm sorry we couldn't get it down to you sooner, but this emergency just came up. Mr. Smith said he appreciates the way you never let him down when these fires have to be put out. If you could give me a ring around 1:30, he'd have a few minutes to acquaint himself with the details before the 2:00 o'clock meeting. Thanks so much."

Unfortunately, there are executive secretaries who have more fun playing "big shot" with the first approach. They deserve the reputation they receive around the office.

When your boss has the authority to get things done, asking in his name is more effective than demanding, in either his name or your own. People may respond to your demand because they feel they have little choice, but they'll resent you for it and they may eventually get even or sabotage some of your work. It's been known to happen.

Over the years, I have known several people who have held high political office. Most of these people are not overly impressed with the authority of their office and are very low key about the authority they have. However, some of the staff people who work for them are tremendously impressed with the power of the office and are nearly impossible to deal with. The elected officials realize how they got there. They worked long and hard to get the votes of the people who put them in office. They realize that the same people can vote them out of office at the next election. However, the staff people were appointed. Unless they were involved in the campaign process they may not appreciate how humbling seeking office actually is.

Assuming the power of the boss's office is a "quick fix" for people who want a great deal of authority but haven't paid their dues or can't get it on their own. The wisest use of authority is an approach that minimizes its use.

If you'll look around your own office or other organizations with which you are familiar, you'll find an interesting fact about some key executives. It's no accident that many of the most effective executives are those who are both liked (maybe even loved) and respected by the employees. The reason they are so well liked is that they are not overly impressed with the power of their office and don't throw their authority around. They rarely give orders. They ask. They don't consider themselves superior human beings. Not all such executives were that way from the start, but they learned along the way that minimizing the use of authority doesn't render one impotent.

Very few people enjoy being made to feel inferior. The problem with using authority or power to get something done is that it may mean you lack other-people skills to accomplish the same thing. It's like using a big stick. It wears thin and may break completely in half.

Many executive secretaries blatantly use the authority of their bosses because they're impatient. They don't feel they have the time to build the people bridges. They have a great deal of work to get done; they'll get around to the people niceties some day. Unfortunately, you may never find the time to be nice to other people if you wait until it's convenient. By then your reputation with others in the office may be so negative that a campaign to overcome it is almost insurmountable.

You may say there are people in the office who don't respond to the more diplomatic approach. That may be true because they have calloused themselves against people who push them around. I will admit there are a few people in almost any office that even Will Rogers wouldn't like, but the majority of people will respond favorably to kindness, tact, and diplomacy.

Your boss will not want you using his power to get things done except under very rare circumstances. Most of the time, he'd rather you didn't try to use his power. If you're having a great deal of difficulty in getting cooperation from another department, he should be told about it, so he can straighten it out with his counterpart in the offending department.

If you find that you are making great use of implied authority from your boss to get things done, examine your motives. Is it because the job must be done and you have no choice, or is it because it makes you feel a bit powerful to know you can push and others can't push back? You may feel that some people respond only to authority, and that if you attempt to use tact, diplomacy, and kindness, they'll walk all over you. To such a reaction I can only respond that someone has to try to break that kind of cycle. The problem with responding with power and authority is that when you react in such a manner, the people you're dealing with are in fact controlling the kind of person you are. It's not unlike someone cutting in front of your car on the way to work. That may put you in such a bad mood it ruins your entire day. If that happens, you have allowed the person who cut in front of you to control your life for that day.

If there are cantankerous people in your office, don't respond by using your boss's authority, at least not at first. Why not try the more tactful approach a few times? They may warm up to you. The pleasant treatment from you may be the bright spot in their day, and it may get unexpected results. Treating others as you'd like to be treated is still a healthy philosophy.

There will be many times, nearly every day, when you'll be making phone calls as part of your job responsibilities. Many of these calls will be made on behalf of the executive. Don't carry your concern about misusing power so far that you are reluctant to identify the fact that you work for the executive. If you're calling the travel agency to get air reservations for the boss, of course you say, "This is Mr. Johnson's secretary, with the ABC Company." Such a statement is not a misuse of power.

If you learned that the last seat on the flight your boss needs was just reserved for a junior executive in accounting, suggesting to the travel agency that Mr. Johnson be given that seat and the junior executive booked on a later flight would be an improper assumption of authority. There would be nothing wrong with telling your boss that the junior executive has the last seat on the flight. If he feels that it's in the company's best interest to make a switch, let him work it out with the junior executive's supervisor. Most executives I know wouldn't even consider trying to bump a junior officer off a flight, but it's not a decision for a secretary to make.

Some secretaries try to bully their way into getting what they believe their bosses want very badly. A secretary might be asked to get her boss two tickets to a concert. When she calls, she discovers that the concert is already sold out. If she says the following, there is a problem:

"Perhaps you didn't hear who I said I was calling for. I'm calling for Mr. Johnson, the senior vice-president of the ABC Company. I believe if you'll check your records you'll find the ABC Company is a big financial supporter of the symphony. If you want that support to continue you'd better find two excellent tickets for Mr. Johnson."

Such an approach is a misuse of the executive's office. If Mr. Johnson wants to call and make such a suggestion, that's up to him. It might even be acceptable if Johnson asks you to make such a threat after being told there are no tickets available, although there are probably more tactful ways of achieving the same results. If a secretary uses such an approach without the boss's approval, she damages his reputation and that of the company within the community. If he makes such a decision and is willing to risk the company's reputation, that is his responsibility.

There are a few executives around—fortunately, very few—who will have their secretaries exert all kinds of authority to get things done. When people complain, they take an "above it all" attitude. They want to remain the good guy who is everyone's friend. When people complain about the secretary's behavior, they appear to be shocked and say they'll "certainly look into it" right away. This is not unlike the doctor who tells the patient to call if there's any problem. The patient finds that it is impossible to get by the receptionist or the doctor's nurse. He or she feels the doctor is a "wonderful person" and the staff is impossible. The fact of the matter is that the staff couldn't function the way it does without the doctor's consent and direction. This may explain why a public opinion poll showed that people had a higher opinion of their own doctors than of the medical profession in general.

A good rule to follow is that if you suspect the person with whom you're dealing thinks you're throwing your weight around or assuming authority you don't have, rethink your approach.

14

Backing Up the Executive

We are all made up of various strengths and weaknesses. When an executive selects a secretary, he hopes to get someone who will shore him up and minimize his shortcomings.

The standard image of the successful executive is either of someone who is cool, calm, and collected, with ice water flowing through his veins, or of a high-strung, explosive personality always living on the edge of a nervous breakdown. There are individuals who match such descriptions, but they are the exception. Another image many employees have of the executives in their firm is one of people loaded with self-confidence. This is not completely true, either. Some executives have a great deal of self-confidence. Others are loaded with self-confidence about some matters and full of self-doubt about others.

An executive secretary can't expect the executive to tell her what his weaknesses are. It's a rare executive who knows himself that well. He may tell her the things he doesn't like to do, which often can be equated with things he doesn't do too well. Unfortunately, many executives have deluded themselves about their strengths and weaknesses, so that they no longer see the shortcomings others see. For example, I know of one senior executive in a major firm who believes he has outstanding "people skills" and yet nearly every other executive in the organization believes his handling of people is a glaring weakness. If this individual were to tell his secretary what his shortcomings are, he would not mention his relationship with people.

Therefore, observation may tell you more than what the person says. For example, many top-level managers say "my door is always open," but their actions give away their true feelings. The door may be open when they are reviewing the department's quarterly budget, but that is not the time to go in and visit about some long-range project. Secretaries soon learn the facts. Saying "my door is always open" but not "always" meaning it is a fact of life and may be an executive shortcoming. When asked by a junior executive if he can get in to see the boss, the secretary will tell him, "It's possible, but he's reviewing the quarterly budget right now. Why don't you let me call you when he's free and can spend some time with you?" Such an approach not only conserves the time of the executive, it also does the junior executive a favor. The junior executive will now be able to conduct his business conversation under favorable circumstances.

Although many executives pride themselves on remembering names, the larger the organization is, the more difficult it becomes to commit names to memory. Some executives want to know the name of every employee in the organization. It's a noble ambition, but it may not be possible or probable. A secretary can help a great deal in such an endeavor. Instead of sending someone into her boss's office and running the risk that he may not be able to recall the name, the secretary merely walks to the door and says, "Mary Reilly is here to see you." With such an approach, there's no embarrassment, and Mary Reilly never suspects that the executive might not recall her name.

Many times, the secretary will be responsible for making the arrangements for retirement dinners or various recognition functions. If it's likely that a large group of people will be there whose names the executive might not recall, providing name tags prevents embarrassment on everyone's part. It'll help anyone in attendance who might not be acquainted with everyone present. It's essential that the executive himself wear a tag, even though everyone knows him. When he puts on the name tag, it says to everyone else, "I don't think I'm more privileged than you."

Many large companies have gone to name tags and photographs for security reasons, but it has the ancillary benefit of having no one forget anyone else's name. It can't solve the nickname problem. If a person's name is Aubrey Jones, you won't necessarily remember that he's called "Doc." But most people would rather be called Aubrey than receive an all-purpose, "How're you?" The name problem is a good example of little ways a secretary can backstop an executive. It may seem like a little thing, but employees can feel hurt if the executive doesn't remember their names.

It may be a matter of preference, but some executives keep a personal book by their phones. In it are the names and phone numbers of people to whom they talk with some regularity. Sometimes the names of the wife and the children are listed in parenthesis under the name and number. This adds a personal touch. If an executive feels it's appropriate, he could say, "How are you, George, and how is Arlene?" or "Is your son Skipper playing Little League ball again this summer?"

The same kind of information is helpful on all the people who report to him. The names of spouses and children can be obtained from the personnel department. If the executive has only a small group reporting to him, he may already know. The problem becomes more difficult as the numbers increase. It may not be necessary to gather such information on his fellow executives in the same organization. There is more likelihood he'll already know the wives and the children, as they may see each other socially.

You may feel this is undue attention paid to nonbusiness

details. It isn't. Business relationships depend greatly on personal relationships that exist. They develop because they are cultivated. This doesn't mean friendship is necessarily exploited for business purposes. It merely means that a business career is pleasanter when you work with friends rather than with strangers.

Often when people call for an appointment with the executive, the request is made through the secretary. Some managers who see a whole series of people in the course of a day may not remember what the subject matter of the appointment is. If this is true, the daily meeting can be modified so that there is a discussion of the appointments for the day. As the executive and the secretary discuss each, she makes a one-paragraph description of the appointment. Later, she types a sheet outlining the time, person, and probable purpose of the meeting request.

This procedure may not be necessary every day, as most executives don't spend entire days with such personal meetings. However, there are times when the schedule of personal meetings is heavy, when, for example, performance appraisal conferences or salary review discussions are held, if everyone is reviewed at the same time of year.

There are two schools of thought on holding all such reviews at the same time. One school, in favor of holding them all at once, notes that you're able to compare performance and salaries of the people working for you. The other school, in favor of spreading them throughout the year, using the employee's anniversary date as the time, finds an advantage in spreading the workload throughout the year. In addition, it argues that evaluating a person on his or her anniversary allows you to compare the person against the standards set for the job and prevents ranking people arbitrarily.

If your organization does review performance and salaries at the same time, you can be of great assistance to the executive, assuming the executive allows you access to salary information. A file folder should be prepared on each employee who is to be interviewed. Included in the file should be a copy of the employee's job description, the last three performance appraisals, and the last three salary increases. Some executives might want all previous performance appraisals and all salary increases; however, this seems unnecessary for a twenty-year-plus employee. What kind of salary increase he or she got twenty years ago has little except nostalgic value. If the executive doesn't maintain or ask for this kind of background material, the secretary might suggest it. This is the type of backing an executive should receive from his secretary.

Many executives pride themselves on being "big-picture guys." They're looking at overall policy matters. The big-picture guys usually aren't good detail people. If your boss is good at making the big decisions, there's a better-than-average chance he leaves details unattended. They can create problems unless someone, usually the secretary, tends to them. This kind of executive needs someone cleaning up after him. The secretary will need an outstanding knowledge of the department so she knows where to turn for some of the details left lying around while the executive is off on another big deal somewhere. In this regard, the secretary takes on some executive functions, as she will play a major role seeing that these details are cleaned up.

The secretary needs to understand how the department is structured so that when she seeks help, she doesn't create some organization crisis by going to the wrong person for assistance. She should seek assistance from the junior executives who report directly to her boss. It is important that she look for help from people in the department rather than outside the department. I don't mean to foster department loyalties as opposed to company loyalties, but it is a fact of life that the people in an organization do feel a loyalty to the people with whom they work, that is, people in their own department. All departments are working for company goals, but your department is "family," so you should attempt to solve your problems in your own household.

The secretary needs to develop a good working relationship with each of the executives who reports to her boss. The boss can assist in building this working relationship. He has periodic meetings with his junior executives, and although I'm not suggesting that the secretary sit in on all these meetings, calling her into a meeting periodically can reinforce the working relationship.

"Jeff, I'd like you to work closely with Carol on this Chicago lease. She's been involved with it from its inception and can save you a lot of time. I'm counting on the two of you to take care of it while I'm gone." This type of approach establishes the proper working environment between the junior executive and the secretary. It can be used on various projects so that in a short period of time the executive's secretary and the junior executive have a comfortable working relationship. By encouraging these relationships, the executive enables the secretary to go to these people with ease when problems arise in the executive's absence. There will be matters the secretary feels completely comfortable handling, but there will be others with which she's uncomfortable. Then she will need to consult with someone whose judgment she trusts.

Let us get back to the executive who leaves various and sundry details lying around for others to clean up. The secretary may be in over her head on some of these. She'll have to count on the junior executives to help resolve some of these matters. The boss may have to be called to be asked what he wants done. A talented executive who is not good at detail himself may realize it and arrange for its processing. However, many people who are not detail persons fail to see some detail that others will uncover. The conclusion to be drawn is that no matter how conscientious the executive might be, if he's good at seeing the overall picture, he may well not be a good detail man. It's like expecting a person to be a generous tightwad. The two traits may be seen in the same person at different times, but one characteristic is usually dominant.

Although it's possible, you seldom see a major executive who is a good detail man but fails to see the big picture. At first blush, a secretary might think the head of the accounting department has to be a great detail man, but these things are all relative. He probably sees the big picture as far as the accounting problems and its tax implications are concerned. He has accountants working for him who are better detail persons than he is. Since the job of being chief accountant is looked at by outsiders as a nit-picking detail job, the false conclusion is drawn that he must not be someone who is good at looking at the big picture. He is, within the confines of his accounting responsibilities. There's no doubt he's perceived as a big-picture guy by some of the technicians working for him even though he expects perfection in detail from them.

We should also spend some time with the weaknesses the secretary might have. The first necessity is for the secretary to be able to admit to herself that she has shortcomings. She shouldn't be like the executive who said, "I've only made one mistake in my business career. About five years ago, I thought I'd made a mistake, but I subsequently discovered I was mistaken."

It's important for a secretary to be willing to admit to herself that she may have shortcomings. You can't set about correcting problems if you can't admit they exist. We're not talking about a public confession of your faults. There is something to be said for keeping them to yourself, because those that affect the work will probably be discovered by your boss in due time anyway.

Let me give you an illustration of how an unwillingness to admit a shortcoming can get a secretary in difficulty. There are some executives who will assume the secretary can perform any task they assign her, until proved otherwise.

Combine this with a secretary who won't admit she can't do something, and we have the makings of a problem. Being asked to put together some simplified accounting ledger sheets might be child's play for an accountant, but expecting a secretary who hasn't had high school bookkeeping to do it may not work out too well. If the executive further assumes she knows how to proceed with two or three subsequent steps, you have the makings of a mini disaster.

In such a situation, I think you have to be completely candid with the executive and say to him, "I have no training in accounting, or even basic double-entry bookkeeping. I can probably record the information if someone will set up the format and show me how to proceed." Most executives will appreciate the candor, because they'd rather you provided this information right up front than have you try to hack your way through the project and do it completely wrong.

Once it's done wrong, someone has to correct it and set up the format anyway. So you lose time by trying to stumble your way through something you don't understand. The executive may discover far too late that you don't know what you're doing. If he needs the information for a specific meeting or conference, there may not be enough time to redo it correctly. There is seldom anything to be gained by trying to bluff your way through something you don't understand. You'll be discovered anyway. I'm assuming that none of your weaknesses is in the basic secretarial skills. If that's the case, you've chosen the wrong profession.

One weakness with which many secretaries become afflicted after they've been on the job for a while is what I call the "palace guard syndrome." They're reluctant to tell their boss bad news or to let bad news filter in, especially if he's the type who doesn't react too well to bad news. Many secretaries mistake a negative reaction to bad news as a personal attack upon themselves. The executive becomes visibly upset with some bad news. The secretary witnesses his tirade and assumes he's "shooting the messenger."

In most cases he's upset with the news; he's not upset with the person who had the misfortune of giving it to him. There are vital pieces of information he has a "need to know" and a secretary who withholds them from him does him a disservice. There's nothing wrong with a secretary telling him not to blame the bearer of bad tidings. Withholding bad news because it'll make him unhappy is like the police having information that your automobile has been stolen, but not letting you know because they don't want to make you feel bad.

There are secretaries who want to tell their bosses only positive things; they'll go to great lengths to avoid bringing bad news. Although being positive is a great trait, it has been grossly oversold as a principle. There are things not worth being positive about. Remember, there's nothing so positive as being negative about a rotten idea.

Another shortcoming some experienced secretaries acquire is a by-product of their strong qualities. They become so adept at the art of anticipation, which we previously discussed, that they sometimes anticipate instead of listen. They'll hear the executive start to make a request. Instead of listening, they'll assume they know what's coming. So they stop listening and anticipate the balance of the request. Often they'll luck out. The anticipation will be identical to the instructions. However, when the anticipation is wrong, the project is completed incorrectly and the work must be redone if the damage is not already irreparable.

The job of secretary to an executive achieves a certain rhythm. Habit patterns emerge. Both the executive and the secretary settle down into work patterns—or comfort zones, if you prefer. I suspect we acquire habits because they have the comfort of an old pair of favorite slippers. There may be nothing wrong with settling down into these habits, until we get to the point where we believe the rhythm or the habit is important in and of itself, rather than recognizing that it's a style of operation. If the style becomes more important than the objectives, we have a problem. Too many people settle into these habits or comfort zones and then fight to protect them like old friends.

I knew of a secretary who always took dictation while sitting at the desk across from the executive. He went off to an "expand your mind" kind of seminar and as a result he came back and decided he had to get out of his rut. In order to think anew, he decided to change some of his work habits, so instead of sitting behind his desk while dictating, he either sat on the sofa in his office with his feet up on the coffee table or paced back and forth like a caged tiger. This radical change so upset his secretary that her shorthand skills virtually left her and she could hardly manufacture a satisfactory letter. It took her two weeks to clear out her mind so she could again take satisfactory dictation. She was locked into a habit. (If you don't think habits can be mentally confining, just try switching to the opposite side of the double bed, especially if you've been on the same side for the past ten years.)

The conclusion to this anecdote is that within thirty days the executive had returned to his old habits and was back to dictation from behind his desk. The point is that the secretary can get so used to the rhythm of the job that she loses flexibility. You can't be a truly outstanding executive secretary if you become so rigid in your work habits that you find it disturbing to have to do something a little differently.

One shortcoming too many secretaries have is what I call the "we've always done it this way" syndrome. This malady can be deadly. Circumstances change; operations change; objectives change. Doing it the way you always did it may not be satisfactory any more. Recognizing that the old ways are more comfortable is understandable. Fighting to keep them that way is a shortcoming that must be overcome.

The most important element in handling shortcomings is to be willing to admit you have some. Without such a willingness, correction is impossible, because self-deception has taken over and is calling the shots.

15

The Art of Listening

I once asked a crusty old executive who still ran the company he'd founded forty years earlier what one characteristic was the most important in an executive secretary. The response of the seventy-four-year-old man surprised me: "Her ears."

"Why her ears?"

"Because the good Lord gave us all two ears and only one mouth. I conclude from that that he meant for us to do twice as much listening as talking. Most of us ignore that equation, but it's a job requirement for a confidential secretary." He still called the job "confidential secretary."

We all might not agree that the two ears of the secretary are the most important characteristic of the job, but the point is well taken. Being a good listener is important in most business positions. It's equally important for an executive secretary.

There are several reasons most people are not good listeners. One is that to many people the most beautiful sound in the world is the sound of their own voices. What we're really doing is waiting for the other person to take a breath so we can say something clever. Our concern is with what we are *going to* say rather than with what the other person *is* saying.

Another reason we don't listen is because the average

human being speaks at approximately 100 words per minute while the average human brain can comprehend at approximately 400 words per minute. There is a 300-word-per-minute comprehension gap. While we appear to be listening, we are constantly being distracted, because the other person's speech speed doesn't require our full attention. We think of other things and may become so interested in our distractions that we never bother to go back and give our full attention to the person speaking.

A third reason is that you can't show the other person how clever or bright you are if you don't say anything.

In an executive secretary, an executive frankly doesn't want a person who is going to compete with him for "talk time." He often needs a person around him who is willing to be a good and interested listener. This doesn't mean that a secretary necessarily should be seen and not heard. It's just that most of the conversation with an executive secretary is work related and is usually a discussion of what is required to complete a project satisfactorily. It consists primarily of a task assigner and a task assignee. If the assignee spends an inordinate amount of time talking, too much time is taken away from the necessary projects. Of course, the secretary shouldn't be reluctant to ask clarifying questions so she's sure she understands what is needed.

Too often in taking shorthand a secretary listens but doesn't hear. This could happen, too, in transcribing from dictating equipment, but is less likely when you can back up the machine and hear the words again. Once the words are all taken in shorthand, if they're wrong, they're wrong. I suspect—and it's only a suspicion—that too many secretaries transcribe words rather than ideas or the meaning of what is being dictated. Although it's important to make certain the words are correct, the secretary must listen for the thoughts being spoken, too. If the secretary transcribes only words, she may miss thoughts. That's another reason a secretary should have a basic understanding of the business of the company. If you don't you may type letters that miss important nuances about the business.

It might be useful to discuss what's involved in being a good listener. The following traits are useful to anyone who wants to improve his human relations skills, but they also apply directly to the executive secretary.

People pay large sums of money to have others listen to them—namely, psychiatrists and psychologists. Many communities have established so-called "crisis lines" a person can call to discuss his or her problems. The people taking the calls offer virtually no advice; they listen. Some religious organizations have instituted prayer hot lines where you can call in and have someone listen to you before he or she prays with you. Further evidence of people's great need for listeners is the phenomenal growth of the radio talk shows, where the audience calls in on the telephone and has its comments broadcast either live or on a delayed basis to what may be a large radio audience.

Many of the people who call these radio stations are rather pathetic figures. They probably can't get their spouses, children, or friends to listen to them. But if thousands of people will listen to them, the great need to have someone listen is somewhat fulfilled. Some of these radio stations tape the comments during the day so they can edit and condense them. But there's a tremendous serendipitous by-product the stations get out of the delay; the people who call in can listen to themselves. These call-in shows are filling a great need for people. What's discussed is unimportant, although the station has to pretend that it's seriously interested in the caller's opinion. Anyone who serves as a moderator of one of these shows for any length of time may be ready for "the home."

All of us, to some extent, have a great need to have someone listen to us. If you want to be thought of as a brilliant conversationalist, become a sincere, good listener. Many people have trouble becoming a good listener because they think they are subjugating themselves to another person. They have the mistaken concept that if you're not dominating the conversation, you're in an inferior position. The person doing the listening has more control than the talker. The talker desperately needs the listener. The listener doesn't need the talker; there are millions of talkers to take his place. Listeners are in great demand; talkers are a dime a dozen.

There are several traits good listeners possess. For one thing, they encourage the other person to talk. When listeners do talk, they don't turn the conversation back to themselves. They continue the line of talk of the other person. They use certain phrases or gestures to signal the talker they are truly interested in what he or she has to say.

Looking at someone who is talking to you tells him that you're interested in what he has to say; that, in fact, you are hanging on every word. Nodding your head affirmatively every once in a while indicates to the talker that you understand what he is saying. Smiling at the same time indicates that you are enjoying the conversation.

What you say can also indicate to the talker that you have a genuine interest in what he has to say.

"That's interesting."

"Tell me more."

"Why do you suppose she said that?"

"Why did you feel that way?"

As a matter of fact, the phrase "That's interesting; tell me more" will make you a brilliant conversationalist in the minds of people with whom you come in contact.

Let's take a typical Monday morning in the office. Which remarks do you believe would be most welcome to your boss? "God, did I have a miserable weekend." "Did you have a nice weekend, Mr. Ayres? Anything exciting happen? Did Skip get home?" It's obvious that the questions are those of a listener and indicate an interest in the other person's activity. It's next to impossible for a selfish person to be a good listener.

People enjoy being around someone who shows a genuine interest in them. If you practice these skills, they'll carry over into many aspects of both your professional life as an executive secretary and your personal life. The interesting aspect is that you can start out using these techniques because you know people will like being with you. There's nothing wrong with such an attitude. You become well liked and they get a companion who makes them feel good about themselves.

Everyone gains from such an arrangement, and although you may have to practice these human relation skills, eventually they'll become second nature to you. At first you may consider such behavior role playing on your part, but after a while you'll be unable to tell when the role playing has stopped and it's actually you. You'll find a great deal of personal satisfaction in being the kind of human being others enjoy being around.

16

A Sense of Humor Helps

At one time, in preparing the order of chapters for this book, I thought that a chapter on a sense of humor should be included, but that it probably should be one of the final chapters, sort of like a fine dessert following a meal. After thinking it over, I changed my mind and decided it should be somewhere approximately in the middle of the book, because if you haven't discovered by now that life itself requires a sense of humor, then life must indeed be rather unpleasant.

I also thought of calling this chapter, "Don't Take Yourself Too Seriously," but decided against it, because it doesn't convey the full meaning I'm after. Many people have learned not to take themselves too seriously, but without a sense of humor their lives become ones of quiet desperation. So it'll have to be "A Sense of Humor Helps."

One reason many of us take ourselves too seriously is because of the world in which we move. It's important to us because it's the one we know most intimately. Therefore everything that happens at our office looms very large in our life. We should try to do our jobs to the best of our ability, but once we're sure in our own minds we shouldn't worry about it. The key is "once we're sure in our own minds." Most of us are our own severest critics.

Of course the work we do is important. If it weren't, someone wouldn't part with cold cash in return for our effort. But we must keep what we do in perspective. It may be important in our office and it may be important to the people who deal with the office, but it may not seem terribly significant when measured against the history of mankind. So when you've had a bad day and all seems lost, remember that a hundred years from now no one will know or care, so why should you let it ruin your year, month, week—or evening, for that matter? Our jobs are important, but let's keep what we do in some kind of gentle perspective.

My previous title for this chapter and the one I actually chose may be incomplete, but when you combine them you will find it's much easier not to take yourself too seriously if you have a sense of humor. Everyone (or nearly everyone) has some sort of sense of humor. It is more keenly developed in some people than in others. Even if you feel that your sense of humor is weak, you can improve it.

Here's a news flash for you that may give you hope. Many people who have a reputation for being funny, clever, and humorously creative don't really have any of these characteristics. What they have is a terrific memory and what I call a sense of "appropriateness recall." They can reach back into their memory very quickly and find a humorous line they've heard or read that's appropriate to the situation. They get a reputation for having a sense of humor and they do have one, but they're not necessarily humorously creative. It's a lot like the difference in musical terms between perfect pitch (which some feel you're born with) and relative pitch (which can be developed and practiced).

So you can develop this sense of humor by reading, by seeing the right kind of humorous movies, and by studying the subject of comedy. Watch people on television who have a reputation for being funny. Watch the people who are "ear" funny. A cream pie in the face or a pratfall might be "sight" funny, but you can never use it in your work and seldom in your social life.

Achieving a reputation for having a dry sense of humor is acceptable. Acquiring the reputation of the office clown is not desirable. I'm sure you appreciate the difference. Being witty is one thing; being a buffoon is quite another. If you have never said anything funny at the office, break into an occasional humorous line gradually, or else they'll want to check the company's water supply.

Many people mistake sarcasm for wit; of course, some sarcasm can be funny, but there's a twofold problem with being sarcastic. First, you achieve a reputation as a cynic (not necessarily a welcome trait in the executive suite) and second, sarcasm is often at someone else's expense. You don't want to become known as a wit who preys on others. That's why it's best to have your humorous remarks pointed inward or to have them neutral in nature. They should be pointed at something or perhaps someone not connected with your office. Trading insults with another person can be fun, but it is not for beginners and therefore should be avoided.

A sense of humor is invaluable in an office, especially when things become hectic and tense. A well-placed humorous remark can relieve the tension. It's like opening a steam valve so the pressure can escape. It's healthy for the individual, especially for the one who is able to see humor in tense situations. Sometimes you'll be involved in a situation where it doesn't seem appropriate to make your humorous remark aloud, but just thinking it may put a smile on your face and keep you from getting a migraine.

We are surrounded by funny situations every day. It takes a trained eye to see them. It's not unlike the beauty all around us. We don't look for it, and we may not even recognize it when we do see it. After a while, with practice and with increasing awareness, you'll see the humor in what goes on all around you.

Finally, there's a very compelling reason for not taking yourself and this life too seriously. None of us is going to get out of it alive anyway.

17

The Executive's Visitors

Some executives have only a few visitors from outside the office and others have a steady stream of people coming into their offices. We're concerned here primarily with visitors from outside. We're not addressing ourselves to the people from his own office who come to see the executive.

Many executives develop a casual relationship with their employees and particularly with their secretaries. I realize this varies somewhat by region of the country. Some executives call their secretaries by their first names and insist that the secretaries address them by their first names too. If secretaries have difficulty doing this, executives shouldn't insist upon it.

The point is that if the secretary does call the executive Lou, she should refer to him as Mr. Tracy in front of visitors. Of course she shouldn't answer the phone "Lou's office." It's "Mr. Tracy's office." She should address him as Mr. in front of his guests no matter how well acquainted she is with the guests. Some visitors may view the first-name approach as a nonbusinesslike way to run the office and gain a negative impression of the organization. Everyone in the company has a responsibility to see that a positive impression is generated.

Most visitors are there by appointment. The day's visitors should be discussed in the daily meeting, as explained in an earlier chapter. The appropriate files should be pulled in advance of the appointment. The executive and the secretary should have a mutually agreed-upon place to keep these files until the appointment takes place. Some prefer an upright divider.

If the executive has a great many appointments they should not be scheduled so tightly that he doesn't have a few minutes to relax between visitors. Having a few moments between visitors allows him some personal time and time to return the emergency phone call that came in. It also gives him some time to glance over the file and get himself in the right frame of mind for the next appointment.

Never show a visitor into the office without asking the executive first. He may be on the phone, or he simply may not be ready to receive him or her yet. Depending on the time of year, visitors may have coats. The secretary should offer to take their coats, put them on a hanger, and place them on the coat rack. When they're ready to leave, she should get their coats. I believe that both the executive and the secretary should help the guests with coats if there's more than one guest.

In some companies the lobby is far away from the executive's office. Again this is a matter of the executive's preference, but most secretaries are notified by the receptionist when guests arrive. The secretary may then take the elevator to the reception area and personally escort the visitors to the executive's office. There may be some guests that the executive himself will greet at the reception area and accompany back to his own office. An executive can't do this very often, especially if he has a great number of visitors, but there may occasionally be a visitor he feels he should personally greet upon arrival.

"Are you ready for the salesmen from the XYZ Company?"

"Not yet, Mary. I'll buzz you in a few minutes and then you can show him in."

If this delay goes beyond the appointed hour, the secretary should say to the visitors: "Mr. Tracy will be ready in just a few minutes."

Some offices will have coffee or tea available for guests. If the delay is going to be more than just a few minutes, the secretary might offer them coffee or tea. If it's only going to be a few minutes, you may offer them coffee or tea once they get into the executive's office. Whether or not this practice is followed depends on the executive's wishes. There is much to recommend it, however. It creates a more relaxed atmosphere for the meeting that is about to take place.

Some secretaries (and executives, too) treat salespeople who stop in like second-class citizens, and I understand that approach for those who drop in without an appointment. However, I recommend you treat those who do have appointments with the same kindness and respect you show every other visitor. Salespeople form impressions of companies, too, and they are a part of your public. They may also be customers or clients of your firm, if not now, someday. Salespeople are trying to do their job, too. The country's commerce would come grinding to a halt without them.

Again, the method of serving coffee in the executive's office is a matter of his personal preference. Some prefer the secretary to serve the guests. In this case, you always serve the guests first and then the executive. You are functioning as his hostess and therefore he is served last.

Other executives may prefer you to leave the coffeepot, cups, and necessary accouterments on the coffee table, so that the executive himself can pour the coffee for his guests. Still others suggest to their guests that they help themselves to the coffee or tea. I believe either of the first two methods is preferable over the third one. The third method is satisfactory for people from within the company who are on a first-name basis with the executive.

If the secretary serves the coffee and the business discussion begins, she needn't concern herself with refills, as they would interrupt the discussion.

Often an executive will have visitors coming from another city, and the secretary will be asked to make hotel arrangements for them. Here you need to be guided by the executive and company policy. For example, you need to know if the company is paying for the guest's accommodations or if you're making the reservation as a courtesy, with the guest responsible for his or her own bill. Arrangements vary so much by companies in various parts of the country that it's impossible to discuss a standard method of processing them. It becomes important, however, for a secretary to know exactly what the company policy is.

If the visitor is paying for his own billeting and is on a modest per diem, you don't want to put the poor fellow up in the presidential suite. It's better to find out in advance just what is wanted before making a mistake that will be an embarrassment for someone. If this requires a long-distance phone call to the impending visitor to determine what kind of accommodations he wants, the courtesy will be appreciated.

Before you call the visitor, acquaint yourself with transportation from the airport. It's frustrating to an individual to come into a strange city and know nothing about the ground transportation from the airport to the hotels. If the cab ride is quite expensive, let him know so it doesn't come as a surprise. Remember, no matter how familiar you are with travel, there are still business people who don't travel extensively and might not travel very often to your city. The thoughtfulness will be appreciated, even if the visitor already has the information.

A secretary should have a contingency plan in case the unexpected should occur. For example, if an emergency meeting should develop in the president's office and the executive is an hour late for an appointment with the visitors, it would be helpful to do something other than let the guests cool their heels. If the executive is able, he should try to get a message through to his secretary advising her of the delay and if possible giving her some idea of how long it's likely to be before he'll be available.

The secretary should explain to the visitors in a straightforward manner what the problem is.

"Mr. Tracy called and asked me to extend his apologies, but he's tied up in an emergency meeting in the president's office. It'll probably be an hour before he's free."

If your visitors also have appointments with other people in the office the secretary should volunteer to call the other company personnel and see if they could move their appointments up to the current time.

If a guest has come a long way and the only person he has an appointment with is the executive, the problem is more acute. First, if the executive can possibly be excused from the emergency meeting with the president, he ought to be. It's possible that his presence is not needed. If the visitor has come halfway across the continent, the president will understand. This, of course, depends on the severity of the emergency. It has been my experience that presidents and chairmen are people of good manners and courtesy and they would understand the executive's need to keep an appointment. However, this is a judgment the president and executive have to make. It is not one the secretary can make.

Some companies have tours of their facilities. These tours can be as short as half an hour or quite extensive. The secretary can usually arrange for a VIP tour with one of the regular tour guides. In many companies, guiding tours is an ancillary duty, so the secretary should talk to the executive in charge of that responsibility. She should mention that periodically her boss may have visitors for whom a brief tour is desirable with very little advance notice.

If you offer the visitor a tour and he or she prefers to sit, drink coffee, and read a magazine, relax and let it happen. Many people look upon such situations as opportunities to relax and do a bit of reading. One thing the secretary does not have to do is sit with the visitor and make small talk for an hour. Most guests will be understanding of emergencies developing.

A negative impression of the company and the secretary is created if several secretaries sit there visiting about boyfriends, husbands, children, or last night's movie on television. Such conversation should be saved for the coffee break or the lunch hour.

The secretary may occasionally have to deal with visitors who are unreasonable. You have to keep your cool. Keeping your cool doesn't mean, however, that you have to put up with rudeness and bad manners. Someone who is rude to an executive's secretary and then comes on as Mr. Congeniality to the executive himself is not very bright. A secretary should be courteous to these people, but firm if their demands are unreasonable.

An example of an unreasonable request would be if the visitor insists that you break into the emergency meeting to inform your boss that the guest is waiting. The secretary should simply repeat, "He knows you're here. He's sorry for the emergency and will be here just as soon as he can." I wouldn't arrange a tour for such a person because he'd attempt to intimidate the tour guide. I wouldn't offer him coffee either. People lose their right to special treatment when they come on with their "ugly act."

No matter how high the executive ranks in the organization, the secretary must never act as though she's the palace guard allowing only the anointed few in to see the king. Even though she has instructions not to let people without an appointment in to see the executive, she must always handle them with courtesy and friendliness.

If you're the secretary to one of the top two or three executives, people without appointments should never get past the receptionist. They shouldn't even get to the executive suite without the executive's consent, but they still must be treated with dignity and friendliness.

The opinion visitors have of your company can be greatly influenced by how they're treated by an executive secretary. If that attitude is friendly and courteous, it will reflect favorably on the organization. The reverse is also true.

18

Making Travel Arrangements

If your boss does some traveling for the company, you may be called upon to handle a variety of travel arrangements. This could include company car arrangements, hotel arrangements, car rentals, airline reservations, and other miscellaneous duties.

Few business trips of any length are made by automobile today. Most of them are made by air. However, occasionally an executive wants to call on a number of company affiliates and the only practical way to go is by automobile. If the company has such affiliates, there are also company cars, and the secretary should reserve one of the automobiles as soon as the trip is known.

Since the executive or the company probably has a membership in an auto club, the secretary should call and have the trip routed and maps prepared. If the executive has made the trip several times this may not be necessary. However, it's still advisable to determine road conditions and detours.

It is important to know what the company policy is on hotel reservations. There are a variety of arrangements. At one extreme, some companies (and some government agencies) provide a per diem for travel and it's up to the traveler to attempt to get it done for that money. At the other extreme are companies who take the position that asking company personnel to travel and be away from home is an inconvenience at best, so it should be made as painless as possible by doing everything first class, with as much comfort as is available. Most companies fall somewhere between these two extremes. The middle ground makes the best sense. You shouldn't expect your people to live at the city mission while they travel, but they shouldn't live like a millionaire playboy, either.

Once you know what the company policy is, you are in a position to make hotel reservations. (There are executives who prefer to make their own reservations.) I'd recommend making the reservation by telephone. Most hotel reservations can be made by use of a toll-free telephone number. When making the reservation, ask for the rate of the room. Some companies have a discount arrangement. Make it your business to know what discounts the company has with what hotels, and be sure to get the discount. Even if the company has no discount arrangement, ask if the rate it is quoting you is the commercial rate. Sometimes all you have to do to get a discounted rate is ask for the commercial rate. This is not as frequent as it once was.

The nature of the nation's economy has a lot to do with the kind of rates you can get. When the economy is booming, there are very few discounts. When there is a recession, you can find all kinds of discounts, but you must ask for them. Again, you must know what the company's attitude is. Some want you to get every discount you can. Others want to keep up the image that they are a first-class outfit and don't skimp on their people. (I have never understood why some equate first class with wasting company money.)

Even though you make the reservation by phone, you should ask the reservation operator to send you a letter or card confirming the reservation. When it comes in, it should be given to the executive to take with him. Sometimes the reservation card comes in handy if the hotel has difficulty finding the executive's name on its reservation list.

It's a good idea to prepare a folder in which you gather all the items connected with the travel aspects of the trip. A second folder can be prepared containing all the business files that will be needed. This makes a convenient separation for the executive as he places the files in his attaché case before departing.

For some reason I have never been able to understand, some secretaries deal directly with the airlines in making reservations. Most companies use a specific travel agency for all its travel service. It costs the company no additional money, as the travel agencies are paid by the airlines, steamship companies, or whatever mode is selected. If everyone in the company uses the same travel agency, the agency has a large financial stake in handling the company's travel services in a satisfactory manner. In addition, it gets to know your company and your people. The secretary can make one or two contacts within the travel agency and can develop a highly satisfactory working relationship. This will be particularly helpful when emergency travel becomes necessary. Most of the major travel agencies have computer terminals that give them immediate access to seating availability.

Another major advantage of using a travel agency is that it has access to all the airlines and doesn't have the same financial interest in your use of a specific carrier that the individual airline has. In some cities the travel agency or the airline will deliver the tickets to your office.

Some executives don't care to travel on Mondays or Fridays because of all the business travel that takes place. However, as flights are cut back because of fuel prices or shortages, most flights are completely booked anyway. This makes it imperative that the secretary book the flight just as soon as the travel requirements are known. In addition, you may beat the next price increase.

You don't need to worry much about the time needed to make connections. The travel agency will be aware of these requirements and will not schedule a connection your boss can't make. He'll miss enough of those anyway because of delayed flights.

You do need to know the travel preferences of the executive. Some executives don't care to fly on small planes used by some commuter airlines. If that is the way your boss feels, never schedule him on such an airline. Some people prefer not to fly at nght. Whatever his feelings about travel, don't schedule your boss on a flight or at a time he's not going to like.

For long trips over several time zones, many people feel they suffer from jet lag. If your boss's first meeting is at 1:00 p.m. on Monday and there's a four-hour change in time, he may prefer to arrive on Sunday afternoon rather than get up at some ridiculous hour on Monday and go into a meeting exhausted and bleary-eyed. There are executives who like to get back by Friday night even if it means arriving home at midnight. Others would prefer to get a good night's sleep somewhere Friday night and fly home more relaxed on Saturday morning. You need to know your boss's personal preferences for traveling so you can make the arrangements accordingly.

It's important if there are other people from the company traveling to the same meeting that you coordinate your travel arrangements with the other secretaries because these executives will probably prefer to travel together.

Many companies who have considerable travel by their executives and other staff are coordinating all the company travel through one person. That one person, in effect, becomes the unofficial travel agency for the company. This system works out very well, but this person, too, works with a selected travel agency. Until the company has a travel coordinator, the executive secretary will fill this role.

There are so many different arrangements available for

car rentals that a book could be written on this subject alone. My only advice here is to use some common sense. Put your boss in a rental car he'll be comfortable driving. If he doesn't like the compacts, don't reserve one for him. The secretary will have to learn something about automobiles. She will need to know that a Corolla is a small car, a Cutlass is a mid-sized car, and a Caprice is a full-sized car. But you can't lock onto these names forever, because many of them change from year to year. I know of one secretary who reserved a Honda Civic for her 6-foot, 4-inch, 225-pound boss because she thought if it was a Civic, it must be a town car.

The other important thing to remember is to arrange for a car rental where it's convenient. It doesn't do much good to rent a car at a location that's a long cab ride away. If your boss is arriving at his destination by plane, he'd like to pick up the rental car at the airport and be able to return it there when he gets ready to leave town.

Some papers are key to a business trip, and luggage does get lost. When I am flying somewhere and will be making a speech, I have two copies of my speech prepared. I put one in my luggage, which I check through, and I carry the other one in my attaché case. If my luggage doesn't get there in time for my speech (which happened once) I have a copy in my attaché case. Conversely, if my attaché case is stolen or inadvertently left on the plane, here's a copy of the speech in my luggage. So, when you type your boss's speech, make two photocopies of it. Give him the original and one copy with the suggestion outlined above. Keep the extra copy and start a complete set of all his speeches. He will refer to them periodically, especially if he's going back to the same group for another speech a year later. (He can see what he said so that he doesn't repeat himself.)

Some executives use visual aids or slides along with a presentation they are making or a speech they are giving. A double set of these slides should be made and the same procedure I outlined for the speech manuscript should be followed. Occasionally, when a large group of executives are going to a meeting together, all the slides, charts, and photographs will be shipped ahead of time by some company meeting coordinator. The slides, charts, or photographs being used by the executive should be prepared in duplicate, and he should carry one set with him. If the rest of the material doesn't arrive, he'll still be prepared for his portion of the conference. Although this may seem like an unnecessary expense, match it against the cost of an ineffective meeting. (A double set is seldom double the cost of one set.)

Another suggestion that may be helpful is to prepare a typed itinerary. This can be detailed or general in nature. It may depend on the tradition in your office. You wouldn't start distributing an itinerary for your boss without his permission if no one else in your company does it.

The advantage of a typed itinerary sent to your boss's superiors and his peers is to let them know where he is and where he can be reached in case of an emergency. I have known of a tragic situation in which the secretary was called out of town. Other people in the office knew what city the executive was in, but they didn't know the name of his hotel. His wife assumed his office had the information. The office assumed the wife knew it. Everyone was sure the secretary knew it, but the secretary was en route by car to her grandmother's funeral in a neighboring state.

A detailed itinerary shows the dates, all flight numbers, airlines, and departure times. It also shows the name of the hotel, along with the area code and the phone number. If the executive's business meetings are away from the hotel, it shows the name of that facility and the phone number. A more general itinerary wouldn't give all the flight information. Some people feel the chance that you'll page someone in an airport is remote. (It happens thousands of times daily, however.) It will show the approximate arrival time and the name and phone number of the hotel.

There are some strong feelings against publishing vacation itineraries, as they defeat the purpose of a vacation. But someone in the organization needs to know where the executive can be reached in case of a genuine emergency. It's not likely that that information will be abused.

An important note: When you are ready to distribute your boss's itinerary, put one copy in an envelope, put his wife's name on the outside of the envelope, and tell him to take it home to her. They'll both appreciate it.

19

The Secretary's Appearance

One of the so-called by-products of the youth revolution of the 1960s was the concept that everybody does his own thing and everybody wears what he wants. It's a right. The selection of clothing, the hairstyle, and, in the case of men, the decision whether to wear a mustache or beard, were personal decisions. They have always been personal decisions. The difference coming out of the 1960s was that many young people—and some not so young—had the idea that if an employer didn't want to hire someone with long, dirty hair, such an employer was somehow infringing on the rights of that person. They wanted to deny the employer the same freedom they demanded for themselves. Because styles change almost by the month, it's impossible to get too specific about skirt lengths, pantsuits, lapel width, and type of shoes. Other books have been written by apparel experts that may tell you more about style than you want to know.

My purpose here is to discuss that elusive matter called taste. Frankly, employers have become a lot more liberal in their attitudes about personal appearance in the office than I ever thought they would. Some companies have established dress codes. This is not easy to do, because there will always be people who are technically in compliance, but dress in poor taste. Many people seem to have forgotten

122

that an office is a place of business. I have been in offices in recent years where I thought I'd accidentally arrived the day the office was closing for its annual picnic, only to discover it looks that way every day.

A few companies have thrown up their hands in frustration and have gone to uniforms. However, there seems to be some hope. The pendulum seems to have swung so far on the side of tackiness and poor taste that it's starting to swing back in the other direction. People are starting to care about their appearance again. Through it all, thank God, a good percentage of the population has continued to care about its appearance.

This chapter is as much about an attitude as it is about clothing. Let me give you an example of what I mean. If you want to see all states of dress and undress, travel the nation's airlines. Yet the fellow executives of the company with which I'm affiliated always wear suits and shirts with ties when they travel. It's not a company rule. It's just understood. Most of these executives follow the same approach even if they're flying on a personal vacation. The idea is that they represent the company, and their appearance might add to or detract from the company's image. They make certain it doesn't detract.

Some people might object to this concept on the theory that it's a form of corporate conformity. But if you really wanted to see conformity all you had to do was go to a college campus a few years ago and see all the nonconformists conforming to each other. We all conform to some extent or other. I made a similar observation on a college campus a number of years ago. Some of the students insisted they were nonconformists. I told them, "I'll believe there's a nonconformist in the group when I see a young man with a crew cut, wearing a coat and tie, and saddle oxfords."

You can't exist in an organized society without conforming to some general concepts. It's a matter of degree. Some young people have argued that clothing costs are so high that they are justified in wearing jeans to an office. Having paid the bills for jeans purchases for my own offspring, I know that they often cost more than casual slacks.

An executive secretary reflects both the company and the executive for whom she works. Part of the impression she makes is from her appearance. The secretary must reflect the dignity of the office. She should not try to look like a "schoolmarm" or an exotic dancer. Both extremes are to be avoided. There will always be people in an office to try out the newest, most avant-garde styles of clothing. The executive secretary shouldn't be one of them.

The secretary should ask herself, "Is the impression I make on people coming into this office a positive one or do I create a negative feeling for someone else to overcome?" The impression is created by personality, effectiveness, decorum, and personal appearance, which is influenced by how you dress.

In a question-and-answer session I was asked if I could summarize in one sentence how I expected a secretary to dress. While I believe I could have done considerably better if I had more time, for better or worse what I said was, "I'd like my secretary to dress like Katherine Hepburn would if she were playing the role of an executive secretary in a current movie." There's no doubt that if Katherine Hepburn were playing such a role, her appearance would be in perfect taste. To my mind, a person who doesn't care for his or her appearance is not likely to apply a strict standard to work either.

I have a close friend who is an executive in another city. He is responsible for hiring salespeople. He will not hire people who are considerably overweight. His reasoning is, "If they can't exercise some personal self-discipline, it's not likely they'll exercise any discipline in their career either." It doesn't even matter if he's wrong. He believes it's so and as a result overweight people don't get hired. I doubt very much if he ever tells them why he's not hiring them, as he's a very diplomatic person—but they don't get hired. I know executives who won't hire an overweight secretary for the same reason. Again, they may be completely incorrect and unfair to the applicant, but the overweight person never gets the opportunity to prove his or her capabilities.

There are hairdos that are appropriate for a night out on the town that are out of place during daylight hours at the office. The same is true of makeup. I recognize that there are some differences in different parts of the country, but when a new secretary appears for her first day on the job she should observe how people in similar positions dress and handle their makeup. In fact, when she first interviews for the job, she can get a good idea of how to dress and wear makeup by observing the people employed in the personnel department

In the overwhelming number of cases, the company recognizes that one of the departments that is a showcase to the public is the personnel department. As a result, the manner in which the people in this department conduct themselves is usually a reflection of the company itself. If the people in personnel wear sweatshirts and jeans, you're probably safe in drawing the conclusion that it's a very casual operation.

Appearance cannot take the place of performance. Appearance without performance will not survive. Performance without any regard for appearance may not survive either.

20

Handling Change and Detail

In 1825 Ludwig Boerne said, "Naught endures but change." If we were to take that quote and put it into today's language we'd probably say, "Nothing is as constant as change." But equally true is the fact that most people resist change. In an office most people want things to stay the way they are. They don't want their working habits upset. This attitude is shared by many executive secretaries. It is understandable.

One of the characteristics or job strengths an executive wants from a secretary is great attention to detail. If he also wants someone who is able to handle change easily, he may be asking for contradictory traits. The person who enjoys detail usually likes to be able to put everything in order. To put things in order, you have to have systems or procedures on which you can depend. To change the systems or procedures at the drop of a hat will not be received favorably, because then there's no standard on which you can count.

People who like things in a constant state of flux or who like a great deal of change are not likely to gravitate to the position of secretary. Therefore, it's possible that the executive who is looking for a secretary who is great on detail and also clicks her heels with happiness every time a change is suggested may be seeking mutually exclusive characteristics.

But changes do occur in the business world, and the executive secretary must learn to adapt to them. It's also important for an executive to understand that the attention to detail he wants from a secretary may make it difficult for her to accept rapid change. The secretary should also recognize that she may have a resistance to change. Accepting the situation may make it easier for both the executive and the secretary to discuss change when it is necessary.

If the secretarial job requires a great deal of structure, the secretary can handle the change better if some formal structure is part of the change. Sudden and rapid change is likely to encounter the most resistance. Therefore, a wise executive will use gradualism as a means of introducing change whenever possible. The secretary can go a long way toward making change easier to accept if she first accepts her own resistance to change. Springing a radical change onto a secretary is likely to set up barriers that will have to be overcome before the change can actually be instituted.

Most executives can accept the idea that their secretaries are less than enthusiastic about change. Their desire for harmony and order helps avoid chaos around the office. Show me an aggressive, highly driven, big-picture executive type and I'll show you a detail-minded, harmony-loving secretary cleaning up after him. It is obvious that these two positions are in natural conflict.

Because of this conflict you'll often hear executives refer to their secretaries as "nit-picking, detail-loving perfectionists." The same secretaries will refer to their bosses as someone who "runs around like a chicken with his head cut off. He couldn't find his coat at the end of the day without me." Both statements are likely to be true.

This difference in personality traits sometimes causes difficulties between the executive and his secretary. These two people should understand the fact that the conflicting personality traits are complementary and should not be a source of friction between them. An executive would be in a lot of trouble if his secretary were also a "big picture" person who abhorred detail. Conversely, the secretary's job could be unbearable if the executive were as devoted to detail as she is, because he'd be out there with her immersed in the details up to his armpits.

It becomes important for both the executive and the secretary to understand this difference and to appreciate how mutually beneficial their traits are. They should not be a constant source of confrontation. The confrontation occurs when the two people never take the time to reflect upon the natural differences and how they are mutually complementary.

We have fostered a myth in this country that the "big picture" person is to be admired and the detail-minded person is a nitpicker or a perfectionist. In today's world the word "perfectionist" is used in a negative sense. When most people are called a perfectionist the term is not used as a compliment. This attitude is unfortunate, because there are people we want to be perfectionists.

When I fly in a DC-7, I want the crew in the cockpit to be perfectionists. When my physician is diagnosing my affliction, I want him to be a perfectionist. I'm not interested in the fact that 80 percent of the people who have this illness usually recover in spite of the pain. When my mechanic is putting new brake linings on my car or doing the annual safety inspection, I want him to be a nitpicker, because my safety and that of my loved ones may be affected by the degree of his perfectionism.

In the same way, I want my secretary to be a perfectionist, and I believe most executives want the same thing. I don't want her to settle for "close enough" on spelling or "good enough" on the appearance of a letter bearing my signature. If she's adding columns across and down for my budget worksheets, getting "within a few bucks" isn't satisfactory. They need to balance.

Speaking of budgets, they are a good example of how an

executive and a secretary can use their differing personality traits to accomplish a task. The executive may determine the amounts that are to go into each account by cost center, but he may have the secretary do the monthly allocations, placing them on the form, balancing them across and down, and typing them onto the final budget forms. He can make the decisions and determine the amounts, and the secretary can take them from that point to completion. Depending on the nature of the business, annual budget preparation may be one of the bigger responsibilities given to an executive secretary. Being a perfectionist is a most welcome trait for this task. As in the budget example, there are many tasks where the executive can make a management decision and then turn the details over to an executive secretary who then can make skillful use of her love of detail.

When you combine the perfectionist characteristic with a resistance to change, you can see how problems can develop. Carrying on with our budget example, you can see how it wouldn't be a good idea for an executive to make the budgetary decisions and at the same time introduce a completely new budgetary format. The budget change should be introduced earlier.

Let's assume the budget is normally prepared in November. If the executive receives word in June that the budgetary format is going to be changed, he will do well to inform the secretary at that time rather than wait until November. By giving her the new format in June, he gives her time to take last year's budget and convert it to the new format. If she is the kind of secretary who can admit to herself that she doesn't handle change too well, she will, on a systematic basis, break the new format down into arrangeable parts. Then she will take last year's budget, which she has already done to perfection, and convert it to the new format. This will enable her to understand the new system completely before she has to work with the next budget. She gets a chance to make the new format familiar and herself comfortable with it before it becomes a part of the operating system. If the secretary is locked into existing systems, the executive should suggest to her in June or July that this gradual process be used as a familiarization method.

An executive who recognizes the need for a secretary who is a perfectionist or a nitpicker should not become upset when she resists suggested changes in her systems and procedures. That attitude goes with the territory. But an executive can disapprove of a closed mind. Some secretaries may carry the trait to the extreme and consider anything new as a personal threat.

One reason perfectionists may be suspicious of a new procedure or system is that it removes their confidence in their ability to be precise in their work. If you have a great need to be exact and you must work with a system that is unfamiliar, it casts doubt about the end result. It's similar to driving to a certain city with a road map that's partly obliterated. Until you've driven the route successfully a few times you'll feel uncomfortable about arriving at your desired destination without a map.

As soon as an executive knows of a change that will affect the secretary, he should tell her about it, so they can determine how they can gradually introduce the new method. Some believe the executive should gradually introduce the change to the secretary. Often this approach, while desirable, is impossible. Another problem with trying to communicate it gradually is that you're communicating small doses every week. Pretty soon, the secretary starts waiting for the other shoe to drop. She begins anticipating what's going to happen next. She starts guessing and she may be guessing wrong a great deal of the time. In addition, a confidence gap develops. The secretary begins thinking "What hasn't he told me yet?" This strains the working relationship between the executive and the secretary, because the secretary starts believing that her boss is holding out on her. Just as she gets something worked out she begins thinking "I wonder what he's going to lay on me tomorrow."

It's better to tell the secretary about the entire change, but communicate it well enough in advance so that she can introduce it gradually herself. Holding back the information and telling it in pieces is too much like a daily soap opera. She becomes convinced something horrible is going to happen; she just doesn't know the nature of the disaster. People have infinitely more trouble with what they don't know than with what they do know, because their imaginations assume the worst.

Another way a secretary can be of assistance is in working with the executive on his "big picture" ideas. She can often ask important questions that probe into details that may not have occurred to him. This depends on the relationship between the two of them. If someone else in the organization is already playing this role, it might be a duplicative effort for the secretary to attempt to fill it too.

It's a matter of getting to know each other. It may be as simple as asking her boss if he minds some questions about "the Smith deal." He's unlikely to say no, but in the course of a few questions, the secretary will quickly learn whether the types of concerns she expresses have been considered. If she finds that they were considered, it is obvious that another member of the management team is playing this important role, and the secretary needn't concern herself with it.

The secretary can give invaluable support for the other changes the executive introduces into his entire department. She is likely to know how people will react to the proposal. As a result she can point out potential trouble areas in advance. The secretary is closer to and has better access to the grapevine than the executive. She may know how people really feel. The fact of the matter is that some people may tell the executive what they think he wants to hear rather than what they feel about the subject. This is unfortunate, but it goes on all the time, and the higher the position the more it exists.

Many people in the organization who work for the executive may be more adverse to change than the secretary, so the secretary's reaction to proposed changes can give valuable insight to the executive. The executive may think he knows what's going on in the organization, but there's a better chance that the executive secretary knows. If the secretary indicates a certain change may not be well received by the employees, she is probably correct. He ought to listen.

Another way of introducing change gradually is with the intentional leak. This is a method some business people may have learned from government. On the other hand, some business people find it an intolerable methodology for their offices. I neither recommend it nor put it down, but it would be foolish to deny its existence.

Another method would be to leave a confidential memo about the change on the secretary's desk. The only problem with that technique is that you don't know for certain that anybody will read it while the secretary is out to lunch. Your boss can route the memo to another executive without putting it in an envelope. Another, more devious, approach is to put the memo in an envelope marked "personal and confidential" but "forget" to seal the envelope.

A more direct way to introduce the change gradually if the secretary suggests there may be some problem with it is for the executive to tell his supervisors, who can start telling some of their key people. This direct approach works, but it's an official method of communicating, and frankly the employees have much more fun finding out things they don't believe they're supposed to know. An executive who doesn't realize such things go on in an office is out of touch with reality. The secretary knows they exist. The informal communication system in the office can be used, and the executive secretary usually knows how it operates.

Nothing in this chapter should be construed as being against change. It's just that human nature being what it is, many people in offices resist change. If handled correctly, the change can be processed with a minimum of disruption. With a little tact, the new system resulting from the change can become so well accepted in a few months that people will resist any modification to what has become a part of "our system."

21

While the Boss Is Away

Many secretaries complain about the feast-or-famine aspect of their jobs. They're either extremely busy when the executive is in the office and have trouble keeping up, or they find time hanging heavy on their hands when he is traveling. The extent of the problem is related to the amount of travel the executive must do as a part of his responsibilities. The more travel, the more extreme the problems for the secretary are likely to be.

We discussed separation of mail for the executive in the chapter on correspondence, but we didn't dwell at that time on the impact of travel on incoming mail. It's obvious that not all mail can be held until his return. The attitude toward mail marked "personal and confidential" varies by executive, but generally two points of view prevail. One point of view is that it shouldn't remain unanswered too long. The other point of view is that if people wanted someone else to open the mail and read it, they wouldn't have marked it "personal and confidential" in the first place.

If the executive takes the first point of view, a decision needs to be made about who will process the mail. Some executives have decided to refer mail that looks as if it pertains to company business to the next ranking officer in the department, who will determine its disposition. Mail

134

that appears to be personal correspondence is not to be opened.

Other executives have instructed their secretaries to open the "personal and confidential" mail and to determine if it needs to be referred to someone else in the organization for a reply. Unless the matter appears to be urgent, the secretary may be instructed to write a short note to the correspondent informing him or her that the executive is out of the city and will reply as soon after his return as possible.

There is no doubt that much of the incoming mail that is marked "personal and confidential," isn't. The secretary sees it when she types the response anyway. However, some mail is truly personal and confidential. You're being asked to respect the wishes of the sender, not the recipient. There is the chance that the sender may feel, "If they don't treat my mail confidentially when I mark it that way, they probably don't respect my privacy in other ways either." However, this is a decision for the executive to make.

All the mail answered by anyone else in the department should be retained so the executive can review it when he returns. The idea is not to audit someone else's efforts or second-guess him, but rather to familiarize himself with what has taken place in his absence. Some prefer not to review all this correspondence in one sitting, but rather to look at it as it comes up with the advances or as additional correspondence is received. It's a matter of personal preference.

When putting mail on advance during the executive's absence, don't have it come up for action his first or second day back in the office. Either have it come up a few days before he returns or a few days after he returns. Advanced mail is a matter of decision. Unless it's absolutely imperative that he see it immediately upon his return, don't schedule it for then. There are usually enough fires for him to put out upon his return without being forced to go through more routine matters. What happens in most offices when the secretary does have advances come up immediately upon the executive's return is that he puts them aside anyway and doesn't look at them until he has disposed of more pressing matters.

The matter of answering the telephone in your boss's absence requires a word or two. People in the office are likely to know that he's gone if the company uses the itineraries discussed in an earlier chapter. Business associates with whom he talks regularly on the phone can be told he's out of the city. If the secretary doesn't know who is asking, she doesn't volunteer the fact that he is out of town. People looking for executive homes to burglarize have been known to call an office to find out if the intended victim is out of the city.

If the secretary doesn't know the caller, she never volunteers the information that her boss is out of the city. Rather, she merely says, "I'm sorry, Mr. Smith isn't in the office right now. May I have your number? I'll have him call you just as soon as he gets here." If it's a burglar, he won't call back. He'll go on to some less perceptive secretary who'll tell him her boss is out of the city and won't be back for two weeks.

For the legitimate business calls that are received, which we trust will be all of them, the secretary should attempt to find out the nature of the call to see if someone else in the office can be of assistance. The following comment might elicit the necessary response:

"Could you tell me the nature of your inquiry? Perhaps someone else can handle it for you. If so, we wouldn't have to delay you until Mr. Smith returns."

If the secretary can transfer the call to another person who can process the matter immediately, that's a satisfactory procedure. However, if you're likely to encounter delays or run the risk that the client is going to be transferred from one person to another throughout the building, the client would be better served if the secretary took the information and had the person who could handle it return the call as quickly as possible.

Don't tell your caller "I'll have someone call you right back" if to you that means tomorrow. Try to be specific, if you can. If you can't be specific, say "It'll probably be a day or so before we can get back to you. Will that be soon enough?" There's nothing wrong with asking the caller if he or she would like an answer by phone or by letter. Many people prefer an answer by letter, but often ask for the information by phone because they fear a two- to three-week delay if they write for an answer.

People are usually understanding of the position the secretary is in. They recognize that the secretary can't control the fact that the executive is out of the office. In most cases, if they seem impatient, it's because they can't talk to the executive. Their impatience is not directed at the secretary.

Many secretaries say they get two vacations: their own and the time their boss is out of the office. Although they usually make that remark in jest, it may be symptomatic of an attitude toward the job that is unfortunate. The time the executive is out of the office provides a great opportunity for the secretary to see how smoothly she can keep the office functioning. Also, if she doesn't believe she will be busy, she could show her initiative and ask her boss if there are any new duties she could take on while he's gone.

If the secretary doesn't have enough to occupy her it's because she isn't trying, or she's the type of person who is so lacking in imagination that she can't see what needs to be done. It may also be because she's the type of person who works hard only when the executive is around to see her. This kind of attitude should be rewarded with dismissal, because a person who acts that way is not worthy of the position of executive secretary. This kind of behavior is symptomatic of a more serious problem. It is a kind of dishonesty, because you are stealing from the employer.

The employer is paying for productivity and isn't getting it. People can easily understand why taking home wheelbarrows is stealing; most don't understand that withholding the productivity for which the employer is paying is also a form of dishonesty.

In addition to processing the mail and the phone calls, the secretary can do the following during the executive's extended absence:

1. *Purge the files.* Too many files are built upon an ad infinitum basis. Discuss in advance with the executive what can be purged from these files and what must remain. Sometimes the purged items can be destroyed. In other situations the executive will want you to box up the reserved items, put his name on the box, and send it to the company's dead storage room. Some companies have an ongoing file destruction program. They may keep items in dead storage for a certain number of years and then destroy them.

Some executives will keep an active file and an inactive file. They'll periodically want items moved from the active to the inactive file. They may not want items of a confidential nature going to the company's dead storage file for fear someone may read them and break the confidentiality.

Many files become dog-eared. The label tabs become bent and partially obliterated. This is an opportunity to put the files in new binders and type new labels. Occasionally the secretary will discover that the executive will have tossed items into the file. They'll need to be punched and placed in the file permanently in chronological order.

Some executives prefer that you save all the items you propose to throw away. He will glance through them before they are tossed, to make certain nothing important is thrown away by mistake. The secretary shouldn't consider this a lack of faith in her judgment. As a matter of fact, it removes the possibility that something will be thrown away that he may need later. It reinforces the secretary's judg-ment and eliminates second-guessing *after* the fact. And two minds are better than one.

There's no more helpless (and unfair) feeling than the one a secretary has when she's asked to find a file that she threw away when she was told to go ahead and decide what could be destroyed. This is one of the advantages of the dead storage file previously mentioned. If an item is in dead stor-age it can be recovered if needed. If it isn't needed before the destruction period comes up (often seven to ten years) there's a good chance it never will be needed. There are, of course, some records that a company may keep perma-nently. They will vary by the kind of business in which the organization is engaged.

The philosophy of the company of the executive will pre-vail on what is destroyed. Some executives will say "If in doubt, save it." Others will take the attitude that if there's no apparent reason for keeping it, go ahead and throw it away.

In order to keep files current, you ought to purge them at least once each year. There may be some files for which a new folder is started at the beginning of each calendar or fiscal year. That constitutes an automatic purging system. The latest two years might be kept in the work area and the others sent to dead storage, where they become a part of the destruction cycle.

Another method of purging that has proved successful in many operations is the rolling twelve-month system. With this method, whenever you start purging, you remove items from the file that are more than twelve months old. This older material is sent to dead storage and becomes a part of the automatic destruction system.

For file purging to be an effective part of the operation, it must be done on a regular basis and the system used should be used consistently. You can't use the calendar method one year, switch to the rolling twelve-month method the next time, and the time after that use a "seat of the pants" methodology.

2. *Have equipment serviced.* If the equipment being used, such as the executive's and secretary's dictating machines, calculators, typewriters, and desk-top minicomputers, are on service agreements, see if they can be serviced while the executive is away from the office. It's frustrating for an executive to come back from a three-week trip and start on a backlog of dictation, only to have a service repair person show up announcing it's time for the periodic checkup of the equipment. Most equipment companies are willing to show some flexibility on these calls.

If the secretary is responsible for minor maintenance on equipment she uses, a good time to pay attention to such matters is when the boss is away. Another example is a change of telephone equipment. This could apply whether the executive is in the office or not. If the secretary receives word that the phone company is installing new phones in the department next Tuesday, there is no problem if the executive is scheduled to be out of the office next Tuesday. But if he's scheduled to be in the office, the secretary should respond, "Would you schedule our installation next Tuesday at 10:00 A.M. if possible, because Mr. Executive will be in a meeting in another part of the building at that time?"

3. *Clean house and tend to office upkeep.* Most of the housecleaning done in offices is performed after hours. It may be done by the company's own maintenance or housecleaning crew or by a contracted service. However, sometimes major functions are performed during the day and are services hired specifically for the work needed.

If the office walls are going to be repainted, it is obvious that the timing of the entire task will not be determined (necessarily) by when the executive is traveling. However, if the secretary learns that the private office walls are going to be painted, recovered, or repaneled during the months of February and March and she knows her boss is going to be gone three weeks in February, the solution is obvious. The secretary should contact the member of the managerial staff who is responsible for coordinating the project and see if her boss's office can be refinished during his time away from the office. It's a more effective use of everyone's time.

It makes no sense for an executive to come back from a trip only to find that on his first day back, work is to begin in his office. One of the duties of an executive secretary is to help the executive make effective use of his time. This type of activity is a prime example. Any time a disrupting activity needs to take place in the area, the secretary does a great service to the executive's time effectiveness if she tries to schedule it while he's out of the area so that he is not forced to try to work around it.

4. *Get a jump on seasonal tasks.* There are often seasonal tasks a secretary has to perform with elements that can be prepared in advance. These tasks vary a great deal by the type of business or industry. You may be involved in annual budget preparation for the department or, if your boss is the company's chief budget officer, for the entire organization. The worksheets, the account titles, and the cost centers could be prepared in advance, so that when budget preparation time comes, you just have to fill in the appropriate dollar figures the executive gives you.

Another example would be inventory. Many organizations do a complete inventory on an annual basis. Some parts of it can't be prepared in advance, but some can. The furniture and equipment in the executive's office and those used by the secretary can be listed at any time. Then it's a matter of keeping a record of anything new or replaced from that point forward. This can be done while the executive is out of the office.

5. *Offer to help others.* One of the more frustrating mo-

ments in the business life of an executive secretary is to have more work than she can handle, while one of the other secretaries (whose boss is out of town) is gabbing on the telephone, reading a novel, or playing a leisurely game of solitaire. This should never happen with professional secretaries.

When the boss is out of town, the secretary should offer to help other secretaries if they get in a bind and can use some help in order to stay current with their work. The day will come when the situation is reversed and the executive secretary will be the recipient of the assistance. It has to be a reciprocal arrangement. A secretary who accepts assistance whenever it's offered but never reciprocates will soon be shut off from further assistance. I think secretaries should be generous with each other, but they shouldn't be stupid and allow others to take advantage of them by receiving but never giving of themselves.

6. *Improve your knowledge.* If the executive travels a great deal, it is possible that a secretary will get all of the previously mentioned projects out of the way. It's also possible that others don't need help. Perhaps some of the other secretaries are caught up with their work too. Several executives may be at the same meeting. Under such circumstances there's nothing wrong with reading a novel or a magazine. Right? Wrong.

What kind of impression does it make on visitors to the area if several secretaries are sitting around reading magazines or novels? What's worse is for secretaries to sit around discussing their children, boyfriends, or last night's date. It creates a tremendously negative impression. It's true that many jobs have some slack times, but an executive secretary is supposed to use her head. Goofing off, as just described, is exceedingly poor judgment.

If the secretary is caught up with everything and no one in the area needs help, the time might be used to improve one's knowledge of the job or of the business in which the company is involved. Books on improving vocabulary would be helpful to any secretary. Depending on what kind of business you're in, there are materials available to teach you more about the products or the services. The more knowledge you can obtain about your business, the better you'll perform as an executive secretary.

You don't have the right to read a novel or magazine. You may think this position is a harsh one, but I believe if you have free time during office hours it ought to be devoted to making you a better employee.

Many companies offer educational courses. Executive secretaries should avail themselves of such educational opportunities, but they should seek the guidance of the executive or the personnel department about which choices seem most appropriate at a given state of career experience and development.

I have known executive secretaries who use such time to write personal letters, write checks and balance their checking accounts, make lengthy personal phone calls, and plan next weekend's social activities. It is improper, and while I'm sure they know better, a major share of the fault lies with the executive who doesn't bother to tell them that he doesn't approve of such activity. If the executive does approve of such activity during office hours, that may make it acceptable, but it does not make it proper.

The time an executive is gone from the office provides the secretary several opportunities. First of all, the pace is not quite as hectic, which is a welcome change. Such a change in the rhythm of the workday is healthy for the secretary. Second, it presents the opportunity to perform tasks that can't be completed conveniently while the executive is in the office. The advantage of this second opportunity is that it lightens the workload at other, busier times. However, to attain this benefit, the secretary must make wise use of the time the executive is out of the office. Viewing it as a second vacation could best be described as a missed opportunity.

Of course, some secretaries inherit a portion of their bosses' duties when their bosses are away. They may be busier than ever at such times. Those secretaries can use the suggestions in this chapter for other slow periods.

22

Reaction to the Work of Others

Many people forget what their intention was when they filled out the application in the personnel department. They were looking for a job, which could be interpreted as a willingness to work, and it's true most people have a positive attitude toward the subject of work. It's not until they are on the job and are exposed to their fellow workers that this positive attitude comes under attack and is often ripped asunder. Soon newcomers learn to work either up or down to the level of the people around them. As a result, the expectations of the executive may not have as much impact on work performance as peer pressure. But the people in the office chosen as models by the new employee may be the key decision she makes, and she may make it as casually as drinking a cup of coffee.

There are people in an office who want to straighten out the newcomers so the new people don't work too hard and make the rest of the people in the area look bad by comparison. The idea is to influence the newcomers as quickly as possible before they start turning out too much work. These people know all the shortcuts. It takes some courage to select better people after whom to model oneself.

A new executive secretary in most cases will find a satisfactory model in a more experienced secretary. Often, she'll be working for a higher-ranking executive than the one by whom the newcomer has been employed. The more experienced secretary may be willing to accept the newcomer as a protégé.

The new executive secretary needs to decide at the outset that she is not going to work down to the average and the commonplace, but is going to work up to the outstanding and the distinguished. The executive secretary must not be overly concerned that the average and commonplace workers will be disappointed that the newcomer didn't agree to work down to their level. They may never admit it, but there will be a certain amount of grudging respect. A tennis player may dislike the fact that she is regularly defeated by a better player, but it doesn't change the fact that the defeated player respects the skill of the winner.

The executive secretary owes nothing to those who do only the minimum necessary to get by. She owes more to herself, her own self-respect, and her feeling of self-worth. The secretary can't feel good about her performance at the office if all she's done is the least she could do without getting fired.

The cynics would say that it's foolish for the secretary to produce more than necessary. They'd reason that the extra effort will not be appreciated by the executive or the company. In some cases the cynics might be right about the lack of appreciation from the boss, but even if they are, the executive isn't the primary person for whom she works. The primary person one satisfies on the job is someone called "self." The person who leaves the office at night knowing that she's had a productive day is a much more fulfilled person than the one who goes home knowing she's stretched three hours of work over an eight-hour day.

Some would say that it's naive to believe or even suggest that a person should produce any more than is necessary to get by, because the boss or the company will take advantage of such a willing worker and will ride a willing horse to death. There's a difference between being a conscientious, productive secretary and being stupid.

Performing the work of two secretaries on a permanent basis, giving up your evenings and weekends in order to get it done, and doing it for a niggardly salary is stupid. Being as productive as you know how, being willing to work the full day for which you were hired, and not worrying about whether you are doing more than someone else is the mark of a professional. Perhaps the reason the country's productivity hasn't kept pace is because too many Americans are concerned with doing as little as possible instead of finding personal satisfaction in doing an extra good job. To the person doing an outstanding job, there is the satisfaction of knowing you've given more than was expected. It is a reward no one else can bestow on you. However, I believe most companies try hard to recognize outstanding performers and to reward them adequately. Of course there are exceptions, but I honestly believe they're in the minority.

Can you imagine what would happen to the productivity of the country if most people were concerned with doing a little extra instead of a little less? The productivity of the nation would zoom and our international competitive position would be improved immeasurably. Everyone would profit from such an improvement. Instead of naiveté, I believe it would be a sign of faith in the free enterprise system.

It does take some courage to ignore peer pressure. Some secretaries may have their bosses partially fooled. They may not know what a first-class secretary can do, because they've never had one. Those who are getting by with shoddy work don't want some other executive in the same wing of the building telling their boss about how productive the new secretary is, because that might put some pressure on the slackers to improve their own activity.

If a new secretary creates such a reaction, in my opinion it's a positive thing. However, I don't believe the new sec-

retary should be combative about it. I don't think you have
to wear your healthy attitude as a badge to remind people
constantly of your superiority. If you take such a superior
attitude you may be asking for trouble, and there's no sense
in doing that. It's one thing to perform in a clearly outstanding manner. It's quite another to flaunt it. People have been
known to sabotage the work of others. If they think the new
secretary is coming off as "Miss High and Mighty" she may
be in for some difficulty. In that case, it isn't the production
that's getting her into difficulty, but her own attitude toward the other people.

In most cases, people will tolerate a superior performer
because they believe she's simply misguided, but if the
superior performer starts "rubbing it in" there's liable to be
trouble. Not all inadequate performers can be fired at one
time, because there'd be too many vacancies occurring at
the same time, even though they might all deserve to be
fired.

A few of the mediocre performers may even upgrade
their work. As a matter of fact, some may not have had the
courage to stand up to the peer pressure, even though they
felt guilty about "goofing off" on the job. Seeing a conscientious secretary performing at a more productive level might
give some others the courage to improve their own
productivity.

For many people—secretaries included—the job is a constant battle between "them" and "us." The battle isn't the
problem. It's the attitude that allows such a feeling to exist,
be it the fault of the secretaries, the executives, or both.
The attitude that ought to exist is one of "us." If people
could look at their working environment as a place to coop-
erate rather than confront, everyone would be more productive and find more satisfaction in the activity we de-
scribe as "my job."

Both the executive and the secretary must be willing to
show good faith. Both must be willing to go the extra mile

without taking advantage of the willingness of the other person. Some people have difficulty knowing where the line is and what actions might cross the line and constitute unfair use of the other's willingness. An example might be an executive with a willing secretary who goes far beyond the call of duty. He has crossed the line when he asks her to cut her vacation short so she can get back in time to total his various personal income tax deductions. A secretary taking advantage of the executive might be one who has been given the day off to prepare for her parents' wedding anniversary and then asks if she could also have next Monday off to rest up from the rigorous weekend. She doesn't want to use a day of vacation; she wants an extra day off. Or she might call in sick when she's not ill, just because she knows her boss won't complain.

Some secretaries use their boss as a father confessor to unload all their personal problems. I suspect that many secretaries do this because it's more fun to talk about yourself to a willing listener than it is to sit at your desk and type business letters. If this occurs, it is taking advantage of a willing listener. If it happens too often, the executive should put a stop to it. However, it's sad but true that many executives are real suckers for a good sob story.

Another trait that some secretaries have is a two-faced attitude toward their boss. They're nice and cooperative to his face, but bad-mouth him to the other secretaries. We touched on this lack of loyalty in a previous chapter. We mention it again at this time because a secretary may react to other secretaries and believe that everybody does that— that it's a normal love-hate type of relationship. She may figure she's the oddball if she doesn't react the way everyone else does. That would be an unfortunate way to react. Relationships that are two-faced, that allow one party to believe he is better than he is, that make one party believe he has the confidence of the other when he doesn't, are dishonest.

A new secretary may come into a nest of cynical secretaries who have bad working relationships with their
bosses. If the new secretary is inexperienced and
impressionable, she may believe that they represent the
norm. Of course, one would have to wonder how things got
that way. Some executives or group of executives might be
responsible for allowing such a situation to develop. They
could even be the cause of the poor attitudes of the people
who are there. In spite of that, the new secretary must give
her new executive boss the benefit of the doubt and not
assume he deserves the same kind of secretary. This is a
working relationship between two people, and it ought to be
given a chance to develop.

The new secretary shouldn't assume that just because
others have a poor relationship, she'll have the same kind
of experience. If she goes into it with an open mind she will
give the right kind of relationship a chance to develop. Its
chances are substantially lessened if the secretary comes in
with some preconceived ideas. If she assumes the relationship is going to be bad, it probably will be. Conversely, if
she believes the relation is going to be a good one, the
chances are substantially increased that it will be.

It is not always easy for a secretary to ignore the standards of those around her. Many people feel that someone in
the area functions as the leader, while everyone else follows. This works fine, if the one setting the standards sets a
good example. If she sets a bad example, she should be
ignored.

One way a new secretary can determine who might be a
satisfactory model with whom to identify is to see to whom
people go when they have a tough question or problem. It's
usually one of the better secretaries. When reliable information is needed, you get it from the reliable and conscientious secretaries.

When a secretary allows the group to influence her down
from the high standards she knows are correct, she is allow-

ing others to control her workday. Having your work time controlled by the company or the executive for whom you work is within the framework of the agreement you made when you took the job. Allowing those who don't have such authority to control your day is an abdication of your responsibilities. Those people, in effect, become an extra set of supervisors. The trouble with allowing these people to control you is that they may not have your best interests at heart. There's a good chance they are selfishly motivated.

The relationship of people in a working environment often becomes unnecessarily complex. Pettiness and personal jealousies too often stand in the way of logical judgment and satisfactory behavior. It would be hoping for too much to believe there ever is a perfect working environment and ideal relationships. We all have to give a little to get along with other people. We can't always insist on having our own way. Compromises are a necessity. But you can't compromise when, in order to be accepted by the group, you have to cheat your employer and yourself out of what you were hired to do. That is too high a price to pay for getting along with people. If you have to lower your standards to be accepted by some group, I'd suggest the group is not worth the price. The dues are far too high for the dubious benefits.

23

Relationships with Other Employees and Other Executives

Much of what we covered in the previous chapter overlaps with this chapter. However, here we will be expanding the people relationships to those outside the secretary's own work area. As has been said earlier, the secretary reflects upon her boss. She is an ambassador for him throughout the entire organization. It becomes highly important for the new executive secretary to develop a professional reputation among all those with whom she comes into contact.

She must develop a reputation for confidentiality. People often confide in an executive secretary. I suspect this happens because people sense that an executive secretary deals with confidential matters on a regular basis and therefore can be trusted. There are many people who have never shared a confidence with a clergyman, yet most would not hesitate to do so, because the clergy have a reputation for handling confidence in a satisfactory manner. People may share confidences with an executive secretary for similar reasons. But if it becomes known that such confidences are violated, the secretary achieves a reputation for unprofessionalism; maybe rightly so.

Many of the contacts the secretary will have will be with other executives. They may outrank the boss, be at his same organization level, or be at a lower level. The formality of these relationships will to a large extent depend on the tone set by the organization. In some companies, there is a formal way of dealing with all these relationships. The executive is Mr. Anderson and the secretary is Mrs. Black and as long as the two work together, that's the way they address each other. Perhaps at a social function or at the company Christmas party, when a couple of drinks loosen the tongue, he becomes Hank and she becomes Betty. But Monday morning, it's right back to Mr. Anderson and Mrs. Black.

In some companies the executive is always Mr. Anderson but the secretary is called Betty by the boss. He may call all his subordinates by their first names but none of them calls him by his first name. Again, this may depend on the tradition built up over the years. Then, of course, there is the highly informal office, where everyone is called by first name.

A new secretary coming into an organization should err on the side of formality. Erring on the side of informality may not be received nearly as well. As a rule of thumb, I believe a secretary should call her boss Mr. Anderson until such time as he requests she call him Hank in front of others. The same applies to other executives in the company. I'm not sure why, but the further down the organization chart the executive is, the more likely the secretaries of higher-ranking executives will call him by his first name. It may be that the secretaries don't feel threatened by him, since he doesn't outrank them by as large a degree as their own boss.

Sometimes lower-ranking executives will play politics, and one of the recipients of special attention will be the executive secretary. They figure she's a good person to have on their side. The secretary must be careful that she doesn't allow herself to be used by these ambitious junior executives. She must, of course, develop and maintain a good working relationship with every executive with whom she comes in contact, but she must be careful not to allow people to use her for their own political purposes.

A new secretary will not know what the politics of the organization happen to be, so she must play it cool until she learns what's going on. This is where having a well-experienced secretary as an unofficial sponsor can be particularly helpful. She will have it all sorted out. She'll know that Johnson and McCarthy are locked in a struggle to become the next treasurer of the company. She may know with what people in the company your boss is competing or is allied in certain causes within the organization. It won't take the new secretary long to find out how the game is played in the organization.

I have known organizations in which these competitions are very bitter; in which regular partisan politics is made to look like kid stuff. When one of the participants wins, it is assumed that the loser will resign in a reasonable length of time and find his position as "king of the mountain" with a "more perceptive" company.

Conversely, I have seen fierce competition in organizations between people who genuinely liked and respected each other, and although they fought hard, they never knocked their opponents. When the decision was made, they remained friends, even though one of them was terribly disappointed. If the loser left, he left not out of any apparent bitterness but rather to seek an opportunity to advance with another company.

An executive secretary must be aware of these political goings on in the organization. Secretaries themselves get caught up in it. They'll be pulling for their boss to get the promotion "he so readily deserves." This kind of faith in his ability and loyalty to him is a commendable trait. When he gets the promotion, it's often a promotion for the secretary, too. After all, if the secretary is the kind of assistant to the executive she ought to be, she helped make it possible for him to achieve his goal. So it's only just that she should share in the reward.

In some companies the secretary follows her boss to his new position. In other companies, he may be moving into a position where there is already a long-term employee as the secretary. She may not be able to do anything about it. He shouldn't and couldn't sack a secretary with thirty years tenure because he'd prefer to bring his own secretary with him. I can't imagine that there are many secretaries who'd want to work for an executive who had so little human kindness. So the secretary may not follow him to his new position, in which case she may have a new executive to train.

Every company has a formal organization chart. Some companies print it in their employee handbook, so everyone knows how the firm is structured. In giant companies, perhaps only the department's chart will be shown. Once a secretary learns her job and knows her way around, there's nothing wrong with asking the boss to see the organization chart. It's a natural curiosity. A smart secretary will not ask where she fits on the chart, but rather where her boss fits in the boxes. Her own position is obvious once she sees his slot.

Actually, there would be nothing wrong with expressing a desire to see the organization chart the first day on the job. Unfortunately, the request might be misunderstood. Hence, if it's not a part of the material handed to a new employee, it's more discreet to wait a while before asking to see it. Some people might think the secretary is scheming to take over the corporation's presidency. She might be perceived as not understanding her place as a new, probationary employee.

The advantage of having access to an organization chart is that it allows the secretary to see how the people with whom she's dealing fit into the company. Many people want to know what the pecking order is, so they can be careful in their dealings with the top-ranking officers. Although this attitude is understandable, the executive secretary should be careful and considerate in her dealings with all the people with whom she comes in contact.

At this point, I must confess that I've been spoiled. In my many years of association with the same company all the executives have answered their own phones. The only time the chairman of the board, the president, or any other executive doesn't answer his phone is when he is out of his office or in a meeting or conference in his office, when a phone call would be disruptive. In our company, the newest messenger can dial the chief executive officer's extension, and there's a better than fifty-fifty chance he'll answer the phone. If the messenger said "Can I see you?" the response would probably be "Come on up," unless the CEO were tied up with someone else. However, I've been around enough companies to know that this kind of accessibility is unusual. In companies in which relationships are more guarded, knowing who you are supposed to treat in what manner may be more important.

After an executive secretary is on the job a while, she will learn an important business truth. There's a formal organization chart that shows the way the drafters think the company ideally functions. Then there is the informal organization chart, which is the way it really functions. This distinction is important.

Under the formal chart, you would assume that the head of the department is running the department. It isn't necessarily so. A subordinate may actually be operating the department on a day-to-day basis. This may be with the full knowledge of the department head, or it may be a situation that just developed out of necessity. People who have been around the firm for a while know that if you want to get something done, it's the second-line manager who can get it done for you.

The second-line manager is aware of what's going on. There may be an understanding between the department head and the second-line manager about what matters must be referred to the department head. Usually policy matters must be referred to the chief. Sometimes this type of situation develops over the years. The second-line manager gets a feel for what he can and should do, and has a similar feel for matters he isn't to handle on his own authority. People throughout the organization soon learn that when they want something done in that department, they shouldn't waste their time going to the department head. Rather they go to the second-line manager. Without understanding the informal organization chart, a secretary wouldn't know how the department really functions.

I have used an obvious example, but most of the time the informal organization is subtler. There may be people in departments who are the experts in certain subjects, and they are the ones everyone goes to for those matters. Where those people rank on the organization chart is of little consequence. The grapevine in the company usually has a fair understanding of where these pockets of authority and expertise reside. By learning the informal organization chart, a secretary is able to do her job better, because she won't waste her time going to the wrong people.

A secretary may wonder if it's fair for people lower on the organization chart to be performing these tasks. Their boss may be perfectly aware of what's going on and may be taking it into consideration in the subordinate's salary. It's also possible that the department head doesn't know or doesn't take the time and trouble to find out what's going on. In that case, if the employee doesn't let it be known that he or she is assuming these extra responsibilities, that employee is losing out. The employee ought to put the extra duties in the job description and they should be taken into consideration in evaluating his or her salary.

Earlier, we touched briefly on secretaries using their bosses' authority and thereby creating ill will for the executives and for themselves. There is another way a secretary can create problems, even though she sometimes does it unwittingly. A secretary may have a difference of opinion with another person in the company. If they can't resolve the matter, she may come to the executive and ask him to make a phone call to "take care of it." A secretary should make certain that she's exhausted all reasonable avenues before asking her boss to use the authority of his office to resolve what may be a rather small problem. He may be able to pick up the phone and settle the matter instantly, but in doing so, may build some resentment toward the secretary in a person in another department who has as a motto "Don't get mad; get even."

There are people in companies who seem to delight in giving other people a hard time. The executive usually doesn't have the bad experience, because people treat him with kid gloves. Secretaries may get it, but it is even more likely to happen to lower-ranking clerks, who are like the old buck privates in the army that everyone kicks around. The reason some secretaries are treated more kindly is because they *will* tell their bosses about the poor treatment.

Unfortunately, many higher-ranking executives are not aware of some of the pettiness that exists within their organization. Even when their secretaries tell them about it, they tend to discount much of it and feel it's exaggerated. If their secretaries ever exaggerate such situations or report them emotionally, they may discount all such future communications even though they may be 100 percent accurate.

Therefore, it's important for a secretary to try her best to report these happenings factually, without exaggeration. An executive needs to know that when his secretary reports such problems to him, they are accurate and not overstated. If someone strikes out at a secretary, mistreats her, or is guilty of petty treatment, it is tempting for the secretary to lay it on thick when reporting it. The idea is to get the perpetrator in as much trouble as possible. That temptation should be avoided.

Report the facts as calmly and unemotionally as possible. Try not to overstate the situation because you may make it unbelievable, even if it's true. The secretary must always maintain her credibility with the executive. He should know what's going on, and it's more difficult if he must sort the emotion from the facts. A good rule for a secretary to follow in reporting a confrontation is to understate rather than overstate the problem. Your boss will appreciate it.

If you're angry about the situation, avoid the temptation to rush into the executive's office and let all eight cylinders blow. Even if you have every right to be upset, you can't make your case as clearly when you're visibly shaken. The executive may notice you, especially if you're sobbing uncontrollably at your desk, and ask what's wrong.

"I'll tell you later when I've pulled myself together. But it's nothing you did."

He'll respect your business judgment for waiting until you are back in control, and he'll be relieved to know that he is not the focal point of your emotional torrent. I know few business people who enjoy being pulled into the middle of some disagreement between two employees. It's bad enough for an executive to have to settle a dispute between two of his own people, but it's worse to have to settle a problem involving employees from different departments. In the latter situation, the executive can't learn the facts and then make a decision. He has to deal with his counterpart in another department. The other executive may be someone with whom he doesn't particularly like to deal. He may find himself outranked. He may find himself dealing with an executive who will automatically come to the defense of his own employee, no matter what the facts suggest. Contrary to what some people think, most people, including high-ranking executives, don't enjoy confrontation.

Of course, situations develop in which the executive must get involved. For him to avoid them would constitute a dereliction of his responsibilities. It helps if he can deal with facts, and if he can have enough confidence in his secretary to know she'll present the facts to the best of her ability, that she's not a person who'll attempt to manipulate him to use the power of his office for an unfair advantage.

A secretary must remember that she may not always be working for the same executive. Someday she may be working for another executive in a different department. Therefore, although she doesn't have to be a "patsy" for anyone, she must not take unfair advantage of people who can't fight back, and she must not be manipulative of her boss's power of authority. Almost invariably it'll come back to haunt her. I honestly believe that in human relationships, for every action, ultimately there's a reaction. If you take advantage of others or you use someone for your own selfish gains, at some point it will react against you.

I once knew a man who was quite selfish in his dealings with others. He took and never gave, unless there was something to be gained for himself by the giving. Then one day, suddenly and with no warning, his wife died. They appeared to have had a good marriage. The man was shattered. It was a traumatic experience. He said "We humans share so much common heartbreak. Why must we constantly hurt each other? That's all I've done is hurt and take advantage of people. There's no way I can ever make up the damage I've done." He went to the other extreme and became a docile, meek human being. Instead of vowing to be a considerate person from that point forward, he spent the rest of his years regretting his earlier behavior.

I may not be able to prove that in human relationships

there is a reaction for every action, but I'm convinced it is so. Give kindness; you're more likely to receive it in return. Be fair in your dealings with others and more people will be fair with you. Give warmth and love and your world will embrace you.

24

An Unreasonable Boss

I would not be so foolish as to suggest that every working relationship between an executive and a secretary will work out. A few won't, and we must face up to that fact.

The burden of proving one's competence falls on the new secretary, because she's the person being hired by the executive. However, occasionally a secretary may find herself working for an incompetent executive, or she may work for one who is technically competent but unreasonable and therefore next to impossible to work for. The secretary can't fire the incompetent or unreasonable boss. We will deal with this difficult relationship here.

Life is too short to continue working at a job that makes you miserable. It may be that the executive is miserable himself because he sees himself trapped in a job from which there is no escape for him.

If you are a young secretary, you may have trouble understanding a sixty-year-old man who feels trapped in a job. He may feel trapped there by the money he earns. He may be making such a good salary (which he needs for his family obligations) that he can't afford to quit. Many executives would like to be like Paul Gauguin, the painter who left France and everything behind and settled in Tahiti.

Even if he has reasons for feeling trapped, there is no justification for treating his secretary badly. I don't think a secretary should stay in a job like that. There are plenty of companies and executives who appreciate a talented secretary and will compensate her adequately.

Some executives are extremely goal oriented. They could be called aggressive, hard drivers, and even combative. They are bound and determined to achieve their objectives, regardless of cost. Sometimes the cost is high. It may cost them their lives but meanwhile they make life intolerable for anyone who has to deal with them. Fortunately, more and more companies are recognizing that good human relations are good business. Enlightened companies send executives to courses in sensitivity training, or to seminars on how to avoid stress, or to courses that teach them how to deal with people more effectively.

I don't believe you can make a dramatic change in a person's personality except through trauma, a religious conversion, or brain surgery. If the executive is hard-nosed and difficult, you probably are not going to change him into Mr. Congeniality. But I think improvement can be made, and perhaps the rough edges can be buffed.

The company must bear the responsibility if it has executives who walk on people. Don't tell me what the chief executive officer says; tell me what he does. If he permits executives to consider subordinates so much fodder to be used up to get the job done, that chief executive is condoning such behavior. In this day and age, human talent is too valuable a commodity to be trampled on. If the chief executive officer doesn't know it's going on, that's almost as bad; it's his business to know how his executives get the job done.

I knew an executive who was an enigma wrapped in a cloud of contradiction. He treated his subordinates as dummies who knew nothing. He always knew what was best. He would argue with them and it seemed no matter what position they took, he'd take the opposite point of view and would argue it to the point of physical weariness. The contradiction came in the fact that his performance appraisals and salary recommendations were fair and bordered on being generous. It was almost as though he were trying to make up for what he knew was his rotten behavior. Needless to say, this Jekyll and Hyde character was Mr. Accommodation when dealing with his own superiors. The last act has not been played out on this drama. It's still going on. Perhaps I can report its conclusion in some future writings.

The key question is what an executive secretary does when she finds herself working for an unreasonable boss. If the secretary comes to the conclusion that she's working under an intolerable set of circumstances, the situation must be improved or the secretary should find employment elsewhere. Elsewhere might be in some other department in the same company or in some other organization.

The first thing the secretary should do is determine if she is overreacting. She should ask herself the following questions:

1. Have I given this job a fair test? Have I been here long enough to make such a judgment?
2. Is my reaction an emotional one?
3. Did he treat his previous secretary as badly as he's treating me?
4. Is there any indication that the poor relationship thus far is temporary in nature?
5. Have I done anything to cause such an undesirable relationship?
6. Is the job market such that I can easily find another job?

I'm going to make a comment about question 6 before we discuss the rest of them. Perhaps it's because of my own experiences and environment, but I don't believe you should ever quit a job until you've found another one. The exception to that, of course, is when you are in a situation in which your health is in danger or you're being asked to do something illegal or immoral. Once you decide to leave a job and look for another one, most of what bothered you seems less irritating, because you know (even if you're the only one who knows) that the problem is temporary.

Question 1: Perhaps you haven't been on the job long enough to make a judgment. Perhaps in your anxiety over a new job, you're reading things into the day's activity that are accentuated because you are so uptight yourself. There may be tension on a new job, but often it's self-inflicted. I can recall the first two weeks on a new job and how I went home with a backache every night. The backache was caused by my own tension. You need to ask yourself if the situation is likely to be better once you've had some experience on the job.

Question 2: Is the reaction valid or is it all wrapped up in the emotion of it being a new job? Is the reaction personal? Would it seem valid to you if you observed it in someone else?

Question 3: The question is not too difficult to answer, unless you're in what amounts to a one-person office. Other secretaries are likely to know how your predecessor was treated. You should be able to discover how most of your predecessors were treated. The exception would be if the executive himself is new with the company. In some cases, if the predecessor was leaving voluntarily, she may be training you. She may be willing to share her experiences with you. It should be a simple matter to find out how previous secretaries working for this executive viewed him.

Question 4: This, too, could be answered by determining how the previous secretaries were treated. Perhaps the first two or three weeks were hectic and then things settled into a normal working relationship. If he never had a secretary last more than a few months on the job, he may be impossible to work with or for.

Question 5: If he's never had a secretary last more than six weeks, it's obvious you are not at fault. However, if he has had a satisfactory relationship with previous secretaries, you might consider asking him what the problem is. Are your basic skills as a secretary unsatisfactory? If it's lack of knowledge of *this* job, you have a right to be given a reasonable amount of time to learn the position.

If you come to the honest conclusion that it's nothing you've done, you must decide what to do about it. You should consider asking for a conference with the personnel director. Approach it on the basis of asking for advice or guidance. In many companies, any employee has a right to go to the personnel department to seek advice on any company-related matter with a guarantee of confidentiality. Some companies even go so far as to have an ombudsman of sorts for the employees, but in most companies the personnel department plays that role.

In discussing the problem with the personnel director (or ombudsman), do so as factually and unemotionally as possible. (You'll note that I've made several references in this book to stating the facts unemotionally. I do so because if you tell your story while crying or sobbing almost uncontrollably, people may unjustly believe that you're too emotional for the job. The situation may be as bad as your tears indicate, but many people will discount what you say. It isn't fair, but unfortunately that's the way many people react.)

The personnel director should listen to your story in its entirety and should ask questions to bring out the full story, assuming he or she is a skilled interviewer. If you have discovered that every secretary the executive ever had had the same problems or that he's gone through a whole series of secretaries, you have every right to ask why you weren't given that information before you were hired for the position. If the personnel department knew that this executive was impossible, it should have given you that information so you could decide whether or not you wanted to venture into the mine field.

You can understand the problem facing the personnel department. The director, as an officer of the company, should know which officers are difficult, but he or she also has the job of finding applicants to fill the positions. The personnel director has to find applicants for all the positions that are open. He or she doesn't have the privilege of filling jobs only for executives that are personable and easy to work with. This situation puts the personnel director in a bind. He or she is recommending applicants for jobs in which they're likely to be unhappy.

How this is handled may depend on the status or rank of the personnel director in the organization. If the personnel director is not an officer of the company, his or her hands may be tied, unless the director has an extraordinary amount of courage. If the director is an officer of the company, there are several ways this kind of problem can be approached.

If the personnel director and the offending executive are of approximately the same rank, the director can go straight to the executive and confront him with the problem. The opening approach might go something like this:

> Fred, we can't keep finding secretaries to work for you. The word is spreading throughout the entire company that you are impossible to work for. There isn't a clerk-typist in this building who would accept a promotion to become your secretary. The applicants we get from outside don't stay. They leave as soon as they know what it's like working for you. I'm afraid that if something doesn't happen to rectify the situation rather quickly, I'm going to have to report this condition to my boss, although I suspect it's already known through the secretarial grapevine. I can't in clear conscience keep sending applicants to you, knowing your record.

Such an opening would probably generate a thorough ventilation of the problem. If there is no improvement in the situation, the personnel director has no choice but to take the matter to higher authority in the organization. It's possible that if the offending executive can't improve his people relationships, he will be asked to resign.

A company cannot afford an executive who treats his employees unfairly and unreasonably. Not only does it become known to everybody in the organization, it becomes known throughout the community. A company that has a reputation for allowing its executives (even just one) to be unreasonable to an employee will be viewed with some suspicion.

Sometimes a direct frontal attack can be quite effective, although most new secretaries are reluctant to attempt it. However, if the situation is intolerable, there is not a great deal to lose by attempting it. Its greatest danger is that it might lead to a separation before the secretary has found another position.

Sometimes the direct attack is so much of a surprise to the executive that it gets some results:

> Mr. Jones, I've only been on this job for six weeks, and I think I could enjoy the work, but frankly you're impossible to work for. Unless something can be worked out rather quickly, you're going to be looking for another secretary. I can't work for someone who treats people the way you do. I don't know what your problem is, but I can't let you make it my problem.

The above is a paraphrased quote from a secretary who was working for a Mr. Impossible. It was such a surprise that it led to a three-hour discussion that went all the way back to her boss's relationship with his parents. I suspect it may have been a rationalization. Nonetheless, a satisfactory working relationship developed between the two of them. He didn't completely change his stripes right away, but he didn't mistreat his secretary. Every time he started reverting to his old ways, she'd remind him of it and he'd back off. If he started on his old ways in front of someone else, she'd give him a look that would pin him to the wall, and he'd ease off.

This particular case turned out fairly well. Ultimately, the executive went into analysis, and although he never did become a Prince Charming, people were no longer intimidated by him. I suspect that courageous secretary saved his career, because had it continued as before, I believe he ultimately would have been forced out of the company. The secretary was the only person in the organization who had ever gotten to him enough to generate a long discussion of why he treated people the way he did. He considered his business world a hostile environment to be conquered. Later, he moved closer to the acceptable method of cooperation, tact, and diplomacy.

Often people believe that the older the executive, the more likely it is that he will be the old-fashioned, autocratic type of executive. This isn't necessarily true. Management style isn't related to age. Some of the more democratic leaders are the older ones. They're sure of themselves. They no longer have to prove anything to themselves or to anyone else. The younger executive may be less sure of himself and as a result keep a much tighter rein on his operation. He will be more conscious of his newly found authority.

If a new secretary has a choice of working for an older, more experienced executive or a new one, she should choose the more experienced one. He could teach her a great deal about being an executive secretary, whereas she would be learning *with* the younger executive. She'd go through his growing pains with him. However, I recognize that positions are usually offered one at a time. An applicant doesn't often have a choice of positions.

When discussing the difference between the older and the younger executive, we need to take into consideration the position in the company. What I've said about the older executive doesn't necessarily apply if he's in a middle to lower management position in the company. He might still be there because of his own shortcomings. He might still be there for other reasons, too. In any case, not all older executives are good models.

In today's society a secretary doesn't have to work for an impossible executive. The secretary must be certain, however, that it isn't her inadequate performance that is making the executive impossible.

25

Training a New Executive

Sometimes, during the career of an executive secretary, she'll have the opportunity to help train a new executive. This opportunity will occur for a variety of reasons. The executive she has been working for retires or unfortunately dies in office. He leaves the company to accept a position with another organization. He is promoted to another position in the company, and for one reason or another cannot take his secretary with him.

Adjusting to a new executive in a position with which the secretary is familiar through years of experience is not easy. It moves the secretary out of her comfort zone. She's used to doing things in a certain way and as far as she is concerned that's the right way to do them. Now along comes this new executive, who questions why many things are done that way.

If the new executive is perceptive, he'll understand the comfort zone in which the secretary has been working. He will know enough to move slowly in introducing change. Unless speed is absolutely necessary, he'll introduce change gradually, so the secretary won't feel threatened by the new incumbent. However, the secretary should analyze her own feelings about the executive change. She should be willing to admit to herself that she isn't too thrilled with having to adjust to a new person. Being willing to admit your feelings and get them out in the open makes them easier to deal with.

There are two schools of thought on how to approach the change. One is to assume that methods and procedures are to remain the same until the executive questions them. The advantage of this approach is that it is nonthreatening to both the executive and the secretary. He may have plenty of other problems on his mind in connection with his new responsibility. He may be working hard at developing relationships with his new superior and his peers. If the promotion also involves supervising a number of people, he may have more new problems than he can say grace over. He may appreciate the fact that the executive secretary apparently knows her job and he doesn't have to worry about her at the outset.

The second school of thought is that the secretary should welcome him aboard and immediately offer to explain any of the existing procedures. The thought here is that it lets the executive know right away that the secretary wants to be as helpful as possible as he makes the transition to his new position. Then there is no doubt in his mind that the secretary wants to be cooperative. However, he may also perceive it as a lock on present procedures that is indicative of lack of flexibility.

I think a third approach has the advantages of both without any disadvantages. Offer to explain any of the current procedures, but don't press it. Say something like "I realize that you have many new responsibilities, so you let me know when you want me to go over any of our existing systems. By then perhaps you'll have a feel of what modifications you'd like to make."

This third approach indicates a willingness to explain anything in which he's interested, but it also shows that the secretary recognizes that he has other things to which he may have to give higher priority. There's also a clear signal that the secretary is not a rigid person who'll fight to the death to hang on to every existing system.

After the new executive is on the job a while, more frequent conversations will take place between the executive and the secretary. Not only will the systems be discussed, but at some time the subject will also get around to the executive who previously held the job. *Under no circumstances* should the secretary ever say anything derogatory about her previous boss. No matter how she feels, she shouldn't verbalize it. He'll construe criticism as a lack of loyalty to the previous executive and will quickly draw the conclusion that if she isn't loyal to his predecessor, she won't be loyal to him either.

If he's new to the company, he'll look to the secretary to help him with the "shorthand" of how the organization really operates. The secretary, especially if she has long experience with the firm, will know how the informal organization chart varies from the formal organization chart. She will be able to tell him who the key people are in the building who can get things done. She'll be aware of the office politics. She should know what the no-no's are. If the chairman or the president has occupational hobbies, she can tell him about them so he can avoid some crucial office faux pas. Many a new executive gets into difficulty accidentally and unknowingly. An experienced secretary can help him avoid errors. A bright executive will be most appreciative of this kind of assistance. It should be the beginning of a strong relationship between the two of them.

The executive who is new to the company will need to know the relationship of the other executives in the company to each other and to the top brass. For example, are there two executives who absolutely can't stand each other? If there are, it's important that the new executive and his wife not invite the two of them to dinner for the same evening. What executives are competing with each other for what positions? The secretary can bring him up to date on all the office scuttlebutt.

If the executive is promoted to his position from within the company, he is probably aware of the inner workings of the office and the inside knowledge isn't quite as vital to him. However, there still will be many aspects of the new position on which the secretary can provide vital assistance.

Even though he has been with the company for a while, the position is new to him. If he is promoted from within the department, he will be quite knowledgeable about its inner workings. However, if he came from another department, he may have considerable knowledge of the company but very little of the departmental workings. In other words, no matter where the promoted executive comes from, either inside or outside the company, the secretary can be of great assistance in getting him acclimated to his new position.

26

The Job Description

Nearly all companies now use job descriptions. Some companies use formal systems and others have rather informal systems that may be little more than a list written on the back of an envelope. The executive secretary's involvement with the job description will vary by her length of time on the job.

When the secretary is new, she will look to the job description as a source of information. One of the biggest mistakes people in offices make, secretaries included, is in believing in the job description as the final authority as to what should be done. If it isn't in the job description, they believe they shouldn't be asked to do it. They have the emphasis turned around. As new responsibilities are added, the job description is periodically updated to reflect them. Under most circumstances, the duty comes first; its inclusion in the job description follows.

The person who doesn't want to perform a task until it's included in the job description has narrowed the scope of the job. An executive isn't going to put new duties into a job description, have it scored by the job evaluation committee, and get an expanded salary range only to find out it's a task that the secretary can't handle or that doesn't work out logistically. Then he's in a real bind, because he'll have to reverse everything. His superiors could rightfully ask "Why did you put it in the job description before you knew that it would work out or that the secretary could handle it?"

Virtually every new task that a secretary has put in her job description is added after both the executive and the secretary know it can be fitted successfully into the job. It's a way of incrementally adding responsibility to the job.

Most companies that have a formal job evaluation system have a yearly updating of all job descriptions. You don't necessarily change a job description every time a new task is added, unless the new task is a substantial change in responsibilities. Admittedly, what is substantial can be quite subjective. The secretary should keep a list of all new duties added to the job and, to be completely fair, should also keep track of duties that are eliminated. Then when the annual update occurs, the revisions should be made.

In some organizations, the job incumbent rewrites his or her own job description, which is then reviewed by the executive. In other companies, the executive rewrites the description and has the incumbent review it for her concurrence. This concurrence should come about honestly. The danger is that if the secretary rewrites the job description, the executive often thinks she has overwritten it or put too much detail in it. Conversely, if the executive rewrites the job description, the secretary often feels the executive has underwritten it and has left out significant elements of the position.

For these conflicting reasons, it's important that the executive and the secretary agree on the rewritten job description. This is a situation in which the executive will do well not to insist that the way he writes it is "final." If the secretary disagrees, compromise language in the description is called for. After all, it's the description for her job and she should feel that what has been written does a fair job of telling a committee what she does to earn her daily bread.

As one who has spent quite a few years on a job evaluation committee, I can honestly say that most job descriptions I've seen tend to be overwritten. Overwriting the job description works against the incumbent's total score. Committees recognize puffed-up job descriptions; they've seen so many of them. People writing job descriptions try to tell a committee how important a job is, instead of what the duties are. It is my opinion that putting too much into a job description works against the score. Stick to the facts. I wouldn't recommend understating. You don't want to overlook something important. But I certainly recommend against overstating. Overstating is an insult to the committee, because it says, "I suspect you may not be able to fit this position into the proper job hierarchy, so I'll help you." Just the facts, please.

When the secretary is keeping her list of changes that occur in the job, she should lean on the side of writing down every change that takes place. If it's too minor to be included, she can decide that at the time of the annual rewrite.

Some of the important tasks not written down by secretaries for the annual rewrite may include the following:

- Being cross-trained with another executive secretary and being able to handle that secretary's work on an emergency basis.
- Getting involved in a community activity as a result of her boss's community service. When the executive becomes chairman of the local United Way campaign, as an example, it creates additional work for the secretary. Many companies are willing to accept these duties for inclusion in a job description.
- Making hotel and travel arrangements for the executive or for company guests. Although many may not consider this important, just foul it up once or twice and you'll see how important it is.

- Taking on additional responsibilities because, for example, the executive is the chairman of committees within the organization.
- Coming to the office with some regularity on the weekend because of emergencies.
- Serving as hostess for company visitors. If these people are the company board members, it might be considered of more than minor importance.
- Traveling for the company.
- Having contact with the public. It may be casual or the company's image may be involved, making the contacts significant.
- Processing confidential information.
- Making decisions in the absence of the executive. She may write letters in his absence that deal with substantive matters.

One way to approach updating the job description is to write down everything you do for one month. You also have to take into consideration items that are performed in some other time frame. At the end of the month, compare the list against the job description. Does everything on the list fit into the existing job description? If it doesn't, it ought to go on a list to be considered for the updating.

A secretary needs to remind her boss that a continuation of little things may add to a significant change. For example, the items added each year by themselves might not be significant, but if you were to take the job description of three years ago and compare it to the current one, the change might be substantial. The reason this becomes important is because some job evaluation systems don't automatically rescore all jobs each year. They may depend on the executive in charge to tell them when there has been enough change to warrant a rescoring. The change in one year may not amount to much, but the accumulation over several years could amount to a substantial score change.

There's nothing wrong in the secretary reminding the executive of this fact. After all, the job description generates a score. The score generates a salary range. The salary range provides the dollars that can be paid. So the secretary has a vital interest in the job evaluation score.

27

The Performance Appraisal

The relationship between the executive and his secretary often becomes most strained over the performance appraisal. If the company has a job evaluation system, it often has a formal performance appraisal system as well.

It is always dangerous to make generalities and I recognize the risk involved. However, the communication at performance appraisal time becomes heavy. The executive can go over ten appraisal factors with a subordinate and rate the employee highly on nine of them. He can show the tenth factor as less than satisfactory, requiring improvement, and the employee will ignore the nine positive traits and zero in on the negative one. The executive may consider the employee's overall performance as clearly outstanding, and give that as the summary appraisal, but the only thing the employee will hear is the tenth item that wasn't too good. Instead of leaving the office feeling 10 feet tall, the employee walks out as though he or she had just received a kick in the teeth.

This kind of situation seems to become even more dramatic with executive secretaries, I suspect because the working relationship is so close. The secretary can't believe he is so "ignorant of what I do that he could rate me that way." "He works so closely with me every day, I can't believe he wouldn't have said something before this if I wasn't performing satisfactorily."

The problem is that very few of us can be completely objective about our own performance. The executive has the same problem about his performance. His reaction to his boss's appraisal of his performance could be similar to his secretary's response.

People adjust their working habits to each other's strengths and weaknesses. This is especially true of the executive-secretary relationship. Often this adjustment is so total that they no longer recognize performance short-comings. They've built little methods to work around these weaknesses, and after a while they no longer are aware that there is a weakness.

An example might make the point better. If an executive hired a secretary whose shorthand was shaky, he might have done so because he thought with practice it would improve. After a while, he learns that it's not getting any better. But the secretary has so many other good qualities, he decides to try dictation equipment so they no longer have to depend on her shorthand. This could be a perfectly rational approach, but it doesn't improve the secretary's shorthand. The job has been restructured around her skills or lack of skills. He might now consider her a perfect secre-tary, and she may be, within the framework of the restruc-tured job, but she isn't if you compare her performance with the original job requirements.

If this secretary's performance appraisal indicates her shorthand isn't up to acceptable standards, a logical person would have to accept that. However, we are not always logical about ourselves. As a result the secretary would more likely react by saying, "That's ridiculous. Shorthand isn't even a job requirement any more." She may forget that her boss stopped calling her in for emergency letters be-cause of her poor shorthand. She may forget that the reason she's handed a dictation belt periodically with only one letter on it is because her shorthand was a failure.

What happens is that the executive also forgets about the shorthand deficiency. This has been referred to as the "halo effect." You adjust so well to the shortcomings of the people with whom you work that you begin to think they are perfect. In our example, if the job had been restructured so that shorthand wasn't a requirement at the time the person was hired, inadequate shorthand wouldn't be an item to be considered in the performance appraisal. But if shorthand was a part of the job requirement and it's not up to a satisfactory standard, it's fair game for the performance appraisal.

How long the secretary has been on the job plays an important part in the kind of performance appraisal she gets. Any manager will accept a lower level of performance from a newer employee than he will from a seasoned employee. Therefore, a rating of "needs improvement" might be perfectly acceptable for an employee who has been on the job two years.

One of the factors taken into account in many job description systems is experience. How long should it take an employee to master the job enough to perform it satisfactorily?

An example of the ratings that might be used in a performance appraisal system could be as follows:

A. Clearly outstanding performance
B. Commendable performance
C. Satisfactory performance
D. Needs improvement
E. Unsatisfactory performance

A new secretary could be rated as unsatisfactory, especially if the performance appraisal takes place thirty days after she starts the job. Some companies rate all their employees at the same time. Others do the performance appraisals on the anniversary date of the employee.

Again, depending on the company's system and the length of time written into the job description, a person with adequate credentials hired as an executive secretary might be expected to be at a "satisfactory performance" level within one to two years. Therefore, a secretary on the job less than two years could be rated as needing improvement without any cause for alarm. However, if the secretary has two years on the job and is rated as needing improvement, there could be legitimate cause for concern by both the executive and the secretary.

Some executives are "real softies" when it comes to doing performance appraisals for their secretaries. They get carried away; the "halo effect" takes over. An executive who is quite hard-nosed about most tough decisions could be reluctant to face up to the shortcomings of his secretary. He gets to know her so well that he can anticipate her reaction. If he believes she'll react negatively, he may not mention the shortcoming in the performance appraisal.

Although this attitude is understandable, it is unfortunate and unfair to both the secretary and the executive. With no communication from the executive about deficiencies on the job, the secretary incorrectly assumes that she is performing at the very highest level. The executive is deprived of the quality of performance the job requires. Most executives, however, will face up to the facts and mention the shortcoming in the performance appraisal.

Students of performance appraisal interview techniques differ on the best way to handle the negative aspect to be communicated. In our example of the nine positive traits and the one negative factor, some believe all the positive statements should be made first, with the negative one mentioned last. Advocates of this position believe the tone of the interview is more likely to be kept at a positive tenor if the conversation starts on a positive plane. Those who disagree believe the positives are likely to be forgotten and the employee will zero in on the shortcoming discussed at the end of the conversation.

The other approach is to handle the negative item first. In our example, the negative factor would be followed by the nine positive traits. Advocates of this approach suggest you get the negative item out of the way at the outset. By following it with all the positive traits, the interview ends in an upbeat, positive manner. Those who disagree with this approach suggest that hearing the negative first, the employee may be so enveloped with the shortcoming that he or she will only half-listen to the positive items to follow. As a result, the employee is still thinking about the negative while being told about those parts of the job that are performed in a satisfactory manner.

You can find some value in both methods. An executive who understands his secretary very well would know which approach is likely to be most effective.

If the executive does want to control when the negative factor is discussed, I'd suggest putting it in the middle of the interview. He can then open and close on a positive note.

There are a couple of comments that may be of value to both the executive and the secretary. Since performance appraisals are usually on preprinted forms, the characteristics to be evaluated are listed in some kind of order. There may be some advantage in reviewing them in the order on the form, with both the executive and the secretary looking at the form at the same time. Somehow, looking at the form at the same time seems to take it out of the confrontation category.

Some performance appraisals become confrontations because of the manner in which they are discussed. An executive may discuss the shortcomings as a personal failing and say, "Margie, you're making entirely too many mistakes in typing the minutes of the finance committee." Such a statement immediately puts Margie on the defensive, as she feels she's been personally attacked.

A better way to open such a discussion would be, "Margie, the minutes of the finance committee have had errors creep into them with some regularity of late. What do you think the problem is?" The latter statement lessens the chance that Margie is going to consider it a personal attack. The executive isn't talking about Margie's errors, he's discussing the quality of the financing committee minutes, which puts the discussion in the proper context. There's no doubt in Margie's mind or in the executive's that the minutes of the finance committee must be improved.

Her boss has even left Margie with a little face-saving device if she wants to use it. She may have trouble hearing the tapes or, if she's typing minutes from someone else's notes, she may have difficulty reading them. There's nothing wrong with allowing people to save face and maintain their dignity *as long as the improvement is forthcoming.* If they save face, find an excuse, and don't upgrade the quality of the product, that is not satisfactory. Face-saving is one thing, alibiing quite another.

It's important for the discussion to center on what can be done to improve the situation. The secretary should try to keep the matter in some kind of proper context. If she's doing exceptionally well on nine factors and needs to show slight improvement in the tenth, she is performing in a highly satisfactory manner. She should react positively. The executive needs to concentrate on creating the overall impression he has of the performance. His discussion of the negative should center on what can be done to make the necessary improvements. It shouldn't be a discussion of the personal shortcomings of the person unless they are the problem. The discussion should be on the work and its quality. The executive isn't criticizing the person; he's critical of whatever work is substandard. That difference is crucial to the executive-secretary relationship.

At one time, I conducted an experiment with several people, including an executive secretary. I had suspected for some time that most people would be more critical of themselves if they were asked to fill out a performance appraisal form for their own work. With one exception, this premise proved to be true. Everyone, with that exception, had rated himself or herself lower than I had in a separate evaluation I did. Incidentally, with the one person who rated herself higher than I had, I went into an in-depth interview about the differences in our appraisals. It opened up a line of communication that might not otherwise have developed.

After an executive secretary has been on the job long enough to be considered experienced, both the executive and the secretary might benefit from each doing an appraisal of her performance. The differences are worthy of discussion. I have found that both the executive and the executive secretary benefit from such a procedure. The discussion that takes place can center on the differences in the ratings. For some reason, this seems to make it less of a personal confrontation, and less hostility develops

Many people don't like the idea of rating themselves. I suspect it's because they know it's difficult to be objective about yourself. (The truth of the matter is that it's difficult to be completely objective about anyone with whom you work very closely, but it's almost impossible with your own performance.) Another factor that enters into the problem is either genuine or false humility. In spite of how splendidly the people may believe they are performing, many are reluctant to reduce that opinion to paper for fear of how the boss will react if he believes they've overrated themselves. There are people who believe their performance is outstanding but are reluctant to say so. They're the same people who'll blush or become embarrassed when paid a compliment. Then there are people who believe their performance is great when it's only mediocre. They create a problem in a performance appraisal situation.

The executive secretary has the right to expect some kind of documentation of those areas in which the executive indicates improvement needs to be made. She shouldn't display an attitude of "prove it," but rather one of wanting to know what is wrong so that it can be corrected. If the executive indicates, as an example, that the letters the secretary is placing on his desk for signature contain too many errors, that is fairly easy to document or recognize. As a matter of fact, the secretary shouldn't have to be told at a performance appraisal conference of the problem. Such information is available as it occurs.

The boss can tell an observant secretary little of a negative nature that she doesn't already know. A serious communication problem exists between an executive and his secretary if daily problems become a news flash in the performance appraisal. A relationship should develop between an executive and his secretary that makes it unnecessary to wait until the official appraisal interview takes place.

Some secretaries believe they should have the right to do a performance appraisal on their boss. The fact is that all of us do appraisals on our boss every day of our working relationship. Some colleges, universities, and secondary schools have had the students do appraisals of their teachers. Some businesses may have tried such an approach. On the surface it seems like a reasonable idea. After all, what's sauce for the goose is sauce for the gander.

Upon further reflection, however, I don't think it's a very good idea. The executive is being rated by his boss, so he is not escaping an evaluation. It may be more severe than the one the secretary receives. What may be worse, as an officer of the company (if he is one), he may receive no performance appraisal at all and may have to wonder how his performance is perceived by his boss.

The danger with rating one's teacher or boss lies in how the results are used. If you think back to your own school days, you may have had the same experience I had. The teachers that had the greatest impact upon my life were not those who were most popular with me at the time I was in school. It took years of seasoning for me to realize who had influenced me in a positive way. Had I done a performance appraisal at the time, I would not have selected those I now consider the most influential. I would have selected those who were the most fun or who gave easy (or no) assignments. A similar situation exists with people for whom we've worked. Those we like the most or who allow us to "take it easy" seem to be what we want at the time. But in later years, we don't recall the easy ones. We recall the people who had challenged us, who caused us to stretch and brought out the best we had.

Therefore, if companies had employees do performance appraisals on their bosses and did anything with them, executives would become politicians and would strive for popularity instead of effectiveness. That might not be in the best interest of the organization or of the people in it. If people in decision-making positions started making decisions based on what would be popular rather than what would be right, effectiveness would be impaired. Sometimes it is possible to do what is right and what is popular, but not always.

I do not mean that executives should ever be insensitive to the people around them or to the people who report to them. There's a difference between being empathetic, concerned, and fair and being easy or a pushover. A manager or executive who is a pushover is often popular with his employees because they can get what they want most of the time. But employees, including executive secretaries, don't respect executives they can manipulate. They don't want such men as their leaders in tough situations that demand sound, quick thinking and decisiveness, because they won't receive it. So although it might be fun to contemplate the idea of filling out a performance appraisal form on your boss, it isn't a practical management tool.

When you ask employees what one characteristic they want from a boss, it isn't being easy or even popular. It's being fair, because the executive who strives for fairness in all he does isn't going to make many bad judgments. On the other hand, the executive whose *primary* concern is being well liked or popular is likely to make many bad calls, because the motivation is all wrong.

Having said that I don't believe performance appraisals of the executive by the secretary are practical, I would also like to say that I do believe it's important that a secretary be able to tell her boss when there is a problem. If his performance is somehow interfering with the secretary doing her job, that information needs to be communicated. In previous chapters we covered some techniques that are helpful in this regard. However, we're now discussing traits or performance inadequacies the executive has that make it more difficult for the secretary to do her job well.

For example, what if the executive mumbles so badly on his dictating equipment that the secretary can't understand what he's saying? There's the obvious approach. The secretary can tell him, "You mumble." This approach might work with some people, but it is not tactful or diplomatic. The secretary is more likely to get the message across by asking, "Would you listen to this one bit of dictation? I'm not sure of what you're saying." If this happens often enough, sooner or later he'll start enunciating better on his dictation.

The secretary should ask herself what tactful way she can get the message across without offending anyone. "How would I prefer to be told, if it were me?" Always lean toward the diplomatic side. Leaning toward the diplomatic side will accomplish a great deal more than leaning toward the "brutally frank" side.

A talented executive who understands himself and the kind of relationship that is needed to forge an effective working climate with his secretary will not wait for her to approach him with such problems. For example, early in her career with the company he should make a statement to her that sets the proper tone.

> I want to do everything I can to help you succeed in your new position. We have an obligation to help each other succeed. If there's anything I can do to help you on your job, I want you to tell me. By the same token, if I'm ever doing anything that makes it more difficult for you to perform your duties, I want you to let me know. It's possible I can do something about it. It's also possible I may not be able to do anything about it, but I can't even try if I don't know.

In my opinion the enlightened executive should set such a tone early in the relationship and reinforce it periodically. The performance appraisal interview is an appropriate time for such reinforcement. After discussing various aspects of the secretary's performance, the executive can ask, "Is there anything I can do to help you perform your job?" or "Is there anything I do that makes it more difficult for you to get your job done?"

It takes an executive with some self-confidence and self-assurance to ask such questions. Many will not ask it for fear of the answers they'll receive. It's the old "What I don't know doesn't exist" syndrome.

In summary, the executive should create a climate in which you can freely discuss those parts of his performance that interfere with yours. If he doesn't give you an opening, you have to communicate the information somehow. Lean toward the diplomatic approach. It'll be more rewarding and, of greater importance, it's most likely to solve the problems and assist you to achieve a better and more satisfying performance.

28

The Executive Secretary as a Future Executive

Probably no person gets to observe and see management principles in operation on a more practical basis than an executive secretary. She is privy to nearly every decision the executive makes. She has the opportunity to witness the gathering of information and the elements that are considered before major decisions are made and implemented.

Many people in the organization work at repetitive, dull jobs, but the executive secretary is where the action is. That's part of the fascination of the executive secretary's job. She gets to see most parts of the executive's position. She is a part of the decision-making process. She sees how every business day is made up of many decisions. Of course not all of them are crucial, but they are like steady raindrops. One follows another.

The secretary has the opportunity to see how the executive does it in a manner that seems almost instinctive. This is why most higher positions in an organization are filled by people who have had many years of experience as a manager, either in the same company or in more than one organization.

If the secretary has the opportunity to work for a top-notch executive, she will work with a person who puts the primary emphasis on his people skills and the relationships with the people in the organization. In most companies, the primary part of an executive's job is working with people. There are many technical departments that can be managed by a generalist who isn't as technically competent as the people who report to him. What separates the outstanding manager from those working for him is his ability to work with people.

I emphasize these people relationships so heavily because there is a likelihood that the secretary may get so wrapped up in the "thing" part of her responsibilities that she won't see the "people" part of the executive's responsibilities. This book, for example, is heavily slanted toward the people aspects of the position. Very few executives with major responsibilities don't have major people relationships. As a matter of fact, the executive who talks about the bottom line as though a series of maneuvers gets one there, and is not aware that each of those decisions has people implications, is the executive who has people troubles.

The secretary has the opportunity to see what kind of people skills her boss has. Unfortunately, not everyone who rises to a top executive position has good people skills. Some people get there in spite of poor people talents. It is interesting for the secretary to observe the confrontations this second type has. In other words, the secretary has the opportunity to learn from both the effective people manager and the ineffective people manager. The latter serves as a bad example.

The poor people manager tries to manipulate people. The good people manager develops a warm relationship with his people. They work together, instead of the subordinate working *for* the executive. The distinction is significant.

If the secretary observes all these people relationships, she will learn a great deal about management. Instead of viewing the boss as the person to whom you react, view him as though you were invisibly standing behind him watching him work. Why do people react to him the way they do? What is his motivation in saying the things he says at the particular time he does? How good a listener is he? Most effective executives are good listeners. They know they can't receive if they're always sending.

In your own relationship with the executive try to view objectively how he is managing you. Do you get the feeling that he really cares about you as a human being, or does he see you only as a machine manufacturing work?

Much progress has been made in recent years in improving the concern management has for the people in the organization. In addition to being good human relations, it's good for the organization. There may still be too many managers who believe their primary function is to manipulate people to get more from them. Some haven't yet learned that there is a better way. The executive who thinks solely of what he wants done makes his own job more difficult. The manager who helps the employees meet their objectives does a far better job of helping the company meet its goals. Having an employee do something because you want him to do it isn't as effective as having him do it because he wants to do it.

If the secretary desires to move into a management position she has an additional advantage going for her; she has been managed. The person who has been managed recently carries a characteristic that is an important ingredient in management—empathy. Too many managers or executives have forgotten what it's like to be managed by someone else.

Another advantage an executive secretary has if she's interested in moving into management herself is that she knows how the informal organization chart operates. She has gotten beyond the naiveté of believing that the formal organization chart really means anything. In most companies, the formal organization chart should be entered into the "fiction of the year" contest. The executive secretary knows how things are actually accomplished in the office. She knows where the real power centers are.

In deciding whether or not to make the move from executive secretary to management, the secretary owes it to herself to take an in-depth look at herself. She needs to analyze her true feelings. For example, "Do I want to move into a management position primarily because of what I perceive to be an increase in status, or do I honestly believe I'll like the responsibilities?" This is an important question to ask oneself. Too many people want to move into the managerial chair because of the status they see coming their way. Status wears thin after a while, and when it's seen for the transparency it is, the job remains there to be performed.

If you want to move into a managerial career because you like the idea of being a manager rather than because you'd like the challenge and the duties of the manager, you want it for the wrong reason. Perhaps I can make the point better with a political example. If a person runs for governor primarily because he likes the trappings of the office—living in the governor's mansion, being chauffeured in a state limousine, and having everyone call him governor—he's running for the office for the wrong reasons. If, however, he's running for governor because he believes that he can make a difference or that the philosophy he represents is the change the state needs at the present time, he's running for the right reason. He can even enjoy the trappings of the office, as most officials do, but it shouldn't be a primary motivation.

There's nothing wrong with wanting the additional financial opportunity that comes from moving into the managerial ranks, but if you find you don't like the job, more money won't be enough. I suspect some of the startling career changes we see in mid-life are realizations by executives that they can't see themselves spending the rest of their lives at their jobs. Many of them have had the courage to make a 180° turn in their vocations. Most have made accommodations in their attitudes and in the jobs so that they find them acceptable. Unfortunately, too many people stay in jobs they can't tolerate and become unhappy, cynical, and bitter people, finding little happiness and often dying ahead of their time.

The point of all this is to suggest to the executive secretary that she consider the move most seriously. Once she makes her decision, she should go ahead full steam and not look back. But before she decides, the secretary should talk to two people: the executive with whom she works and a confidant in the personnel department.

The executive is a good sounding board. In most cases, he'll be willing to be of assistance, especially if he agrees that the secretary is managerial material. Every executive likes the idea of being a developer of managerial talent. He may also be able to provide some insight into the strengths and problems that may exist in the transition. For example, nearly all executive secretaries become proficient at handling detail. Some have a natural inclination for detail. They love it. As a result, a transition might have to be made. Can the executive secretary, as a manager, lay aside a love of detail, step back, and be able to see the overall picture?

In addition, the executive might be willing to sponsor the secretary into her first managerial position. If this occurs, the secretary shouldn't feel she's had an advantage others haven't had. She's earned it by doing an outstanding job as an executive secretary.

The reason for talking to a confidant in the personnel department is that she can have herself tested for management potential. When the secretary was hired, the various aptitude tests were related to the secretarial position for which she applied. She was tested to make certain she could handle the typing and shorthand. There may also have been some basic math and filing aptitude testing. An altogether different set of aptitude tests is used for potential executives. In some companies, psychological testing is done for management applicants. The secretary should ask to be measured on all the pertinent devices before pursuing a managerial career. Often this can be done quietly. I'd recommend doing it even before having an in-depth session with the boss.

There are sound reasons for requesting such testing. The secretary owes it to herself to see how she measures up on these devices, because she won't move into a major managerial position without the company having such an inventory. There's no sense in being made the supervisor of the secretarial pool if there's no chance of ever moving up the managerial ladder. The management testing will provide the information needed to make a judgment. By knowing that she's as qualified as anyone else entering the management scene, she should gain confidence.

Many larger companies have management development programs. There's no reason an executive secretary can't enter these programs, especially if she can do well on the same tests as those to which management recruits are subjected.

There are still companies that enter only people with college degrees into management development programs. Many companies have modified their positions so that candidates with ability but without a degree can be considered. If the secretary lacks the degree, she may more than compensate for it by her company experience, knowledge, and insight into the managerial process. The college degree is an accomplishment, but many people who aren't very bright somehow get through college. More companies are starting to recognize that a person who is informally educated may be as bright as (or brighter than) one who has had a formal education.

I am not knocking education. Everyone should seek a formal education and go as far as he or she can. Some companies take the easy way out and hire only college graduates for their management development programs. They are assured that the applicant has at least met the minimum requirements of the college or university that awarded the sheepskin. They don't have to find out for themselves that such minimum standards can be met. Unfortunately, they are depriving themselves of many talented people who could do an outstanding job for them.

If you are an executive secretary without a four-year degree and you aspire to move into the managerial ranks, don't let the lack of a degree kill your aspirations. Many top executives in this country never finished college. As a matter of fact, a psychologist whom I respect once told me that someone without a college degree competing with people who have a sheepskin may be motivated to outperform his or her more educated rival. It may cause you to excel, because you feel you have to prove your ability.

During my lifetime, I've had several friends and acquaintances who had outstanding vocabularies. None of them was a college graduate. It may have been their method of compensating. (One overcompensated to the extent that you could hardly understand him. He never used a simple word if a four-syllable one would do.) My own father, whose formal education stopped at the eighth grade, had a vocabulary that would be the envy of most English professors. He was exceedingly well read. A well-known American poet who has taught at several major universities is without a college degree of his own. It doesn't change the creative talent he has or the knowledge he can impart.

Mortimer Adler, the great American philosopher, lacks a high school diploma because he didn't complete the school's physical education requirements. I doubt if anyone would find any of his writings less profound because he isn't a high school graduate. If you consider the lack of a degree an encumbrance to your managerial ambitions, the limitation may be primarily in your own mind. Of course, you could always go back to school.

If you're interested in moving into the managerial ranks, read some books on the managerial process. Stick with the basic information. Too many management books make the managerial process much more complicated than it needs to be. Most managers who fail do so because they get away from the fundamentals. When they get into trouble, too often they try to solve their problems by looking at even more complex approaches to management instead of going back to the fundamentals.

It is helpful in any position, but especially if you're interested in the management path, to become a student of human nature. It can be one of the most valuable assets you can achieve. Most highly successful executives have a keen insight into people. In fact, I doubt if a person can be a complete executive without such insight.

Become an avid reader. Too many executives read only business books. You learn about human nature by reading outstanding novels. Most successful writers of fiction are successful because of their knowledge of and feeling for the human condition. Read some poetry, too. It's food for the soul.

It is highly doubtful that you'll talk to your friend in the personnel department and the executive you work for one day, and start moving into a managerial training program the next day. Quite some time may elapse before your opportunity comes. Make use of the time. If, in the testing and interviews, you discover some knowledge deficiencies, you might start filling in the gaps. If you need more accounting knowledge than you have, sign up for a class in accounting at the local community college or university. This action also lets your boss and the personnel department know you're serious about your career ambitions. It tells people your interest is more than a mere whim.

You may find people in the organization who put you down for wanting to move into management. They may be fellow executive secretaries. That's fine if they don't choose the same career path that you do. To each his own.

When they give you all the arguments against it, remember they are probably trying to convince themselves. They may feel once a secretary, always a secretary. It doesn't have to be that way if you don't want it to be.

Even your boss may be surprised by your desire to move into management. The thought simply may not have occurred to him. If he acts surprised, don't take it as a negative response. Give him a chance to think about it. He has shortcomings too. He may not want to lose you as a secretary. Although that is a selfish attitude, it's an understandable one.

If you believe you are executive material, don't let anyone deter you until you've given it a fair shot. Most great accomplishments start with people believing they can achieve their dreams. I doubt if the reverse is true; no one accomplishes much who dreams little. That may be described as a keen grasp of the obvious, but it's important that you not spend your life regretting that you didn't give your dream its opportunity.

But be honest with yourself. Sometimes we believe we want something and on closer examination are not so sure. There's nothing wrong with changing your mind. We sometimes stick with a cause long after our conviction is gone, because we're worried about what others may think. Spending a lifetime in a career because of other people's opinions is the height of folly. However, the executive secretary can begin by asking herself, "Would I enjoy doing what my boss does? Would I find it challenging and stimulating? Would I feel I'm making a contribution?"

The purpose of most management development programs is to take people who want to be managers or executives, train them, give them some experience, and move them into management positions. But there is another aspect of the program. The company wants to see if the trainees have the stuff to move into management. While people are in such programs the organization is constantly evaluating them. Without saying so, the trainees are also constantly evaluating whether or not they still want to become part of management. Some of them leave, and for them that's usually the right thing to do. It isn't the career they want and it's better for them to find out before they're too deeply committed.

Very few of us end up in the careers we thought we wanted when we first entered the nation's labor force. Many have made changes along the way that ultimately led us to our life's work. Many, of course, have yet to determine what their life work is going to be. The important point is to seek a career that is right for you. It doesn't matter whether it's right for anyone else. If you believe you'd like to move into management, several years' experience as an executive secretary is a great foundation.

29

Conclusion

You and I have been through many thought processes since
you decided to spend some time with me. There are a few
more thoughts I'd like to express as we part.

I must admit to you that writing this book has been a
learning experience for me. I have worked many years as
an executive, but I have never been an executive secretary.
The book was written from the viewpoint of what an executive expects from an executive secretary. I hope that if an
executive gives this book to a secretary to read, he too will
read it. He may come away from it with an increased respect for the multitude of duties that an executive secretary
is expected to perform. As author of this book, I wrote
nothing that was new to me, but when I put it all together I
was overwhelmed by everything we expect a secretary to
do and to do well.

Many jobs require common sense, but if there's one job
that personifies the necessity for common sense it's that of
the executive secretary. Common sense is one of the greatest attributes a human being can possess. It's unfortunate
that the word "common" is used, because there's nothing
very common about it. I know of no place it is taught, but
you can't be a successful executive secretary without it.
I'm not even sure you can learn it if you don't have it.

The executive secretary must be friendly and pleasant to

company clients who may be rude or in other ways act in an unpleasant manner. She must resist the temptation to tell an obnoxious client to go to hell. She must be pleasant to the newly promoted junior executive who thinks he's God's answer to the corporate world. She must have the patience of a saint in dealing with these people, because she is a goodwill ambassador for the executive and the company. She can quietly cheer when the executive decides that the company doesn't need clients that badly and tells them where to go.

The executive can be forgetful, but the executive secretary can't be. If they both forget the important file that's needed, he doesn't complete his task successfully and there's been an unnecessary breakdown. The executive can be so pressed for time that he doesn't read the mail he's signing. The secretary can't be so pressed for time that she doesn't proofread the letters, because if a sloppy letter goes out over the boss's signature, it can be embarrassing to the company and to the executive.

The executive's mind can be deeply engrossed in bigger problems, but the executive secretary cannot daydream, because she's the court of last resort. Unless she has an assistant, there's no one to inspect her work. If the executive inspects her work too closely, he's a tyrant and impossible to work with.

The executive's instructions may be incomplete, but the secretary needs to know what he really means. A course in mind reading is helpful. Conversely, what she says must be precise and not subject to misinterpretation, because she represents the executive. An executive secretary can be successful with a mediocre executive. It is doubtful that a talented executive can overcome a mediocre secretary.

The executive can be made to look more efficient than he is with the dedication of a talented secretary. Perhaps the most important interchange that occurs between the executive and the executive secretary is the interview, when the secretary applies for the position. Skills alone are not enough. The chemistry between the two people must be right for both. Although the interview apparently consists of the executive considering the applicant, they are in fact considering each other. If the secretarial applicant feels the executive is arrogant or in any way has the kind of personality she couldn't endure every day, she shouldn't accept the job. If the executive feels that this is not a person who can spend most of her workday performing tasks that make the executive look good and that she would resent the relationship, he shouldn't hire her.

I can recall instances in my own life when I have declined to hire an applicant who had outstanding technical credentials for the job, but whose attitude didn't sit well with me. I recall one who let me know how grateful I'd be because of how talented an executive secretary she was. If I was going to be told how fortunate I was before she ever started the job, I could imagine the kind of chatter I was going to get after she felt we were better acquainted. If I was going to be grateful, I wanted it to be my idea. A little false humility would have been appreciated there. I hired a secretary with less talent but a better attitude, and we got along just fine.

In the relationship between executive and secretary, it helps if both can be honest with each other. Little things can destroy trust and the relationship. I've seen executives walk up to their secretaries' desks only to have the secretaries hurriedly cover up personal letters they were writing. Executives are usually observant people, and this kind of sophomoric behavior breaks down trust. If a secretary has to cover up a letter, it's an indication she didn't believe she ought to be writing it. If she had that feeling, it's because she knew she was wrong. Otherwise she wouldn't try to hide the letter.

It also breaks down trust when the secretary stretches the work to fill the time. An experienced executive knows approximately how long it takes to perform certain tasks. If the sum of an hour's work is one letter consisting of two brief paragraphs, the executive is bright enough to know the secretary's been stretching.

Very few people, not even executives, go at 100 percent of their working capacity every hour of the day. Most people work at anywhere from 50 to 80 percent of capacity. (That estimate is my best guess and cannot be proved.) Although I'm not certain what we should expect, my inclination is to lean closer to the 80 percent than the 50 percent. I'm afraid in practice it's closer to 50 percent. A person couldn't work at 100 percent of capacity all the time without burning out. Therefore I see nothing wrong with holding some energy in reserve for those times when you have to go all out. But too many employees (including secretaries) try to have their bosses believe they're working at full steam when they're not. They are assuming that the executive is naive and that he got to his position in the organization through blind luck.

Here's the kind of candor most executives find refreshing. "Mr. Grovner, I'm all caught up with my work. All the filing you ask about yesterday is taken care of. Do you have anything you want me to do?" If he answers "No," the secretary goes on, "Well, I've checked with the other secretaries in the area and they are fairly well caught up, too. It's only about half an hour until I go to lunch, so if you don't have anything I'll sit at my desk and write a personal letter."

Admittedly this kind of conversation could only take place in the early months of a relationship between an executive secretary and her boss. Unfortunately, in most relationships it never takes place at all. The secretary never tells her boss she's caught up with her work and never asks for additional tasks. In the ideal working relationship the proper attitudes are demonstrated in the first few months.

After the secretary has developed the proper working relationship, she's likely to say simply, "Do you have anything you'd like me to do? I'm caught up." If the answer is "No," the secretary knows she's expected to see if there's other work in the area. If she still finds nothing to do, she knows from previous situations whether or not the executive minds her writing a personal letter.

One reason—I suspect the main reason—most employees dislike work measurement is not because they find it dehumanizing, but because it'll show them working at such a low percentage of their capabilities.

What I'm attempting to emphasize again in the final pages of this book is the development of a solid working relationship between the executive and the secretary. This requires an effort by both people, not just the secretary. The burden appears to be more on the secretary because she's the new kid on the block and she's the one going through the probationary period. In spite of that, it requires an equal effort by the executive. You can't develop a solid relationship with another human being if only one person makes an effort. Both have to work at it.

Too many executives take the attitude that ". . . she's the one on trial, not me." It's true, the executive is not on trial, but he must work at developing the relationship. He shouldn't take the attitude that he's going to treat her just the way he did his previous secretary and she'll have to adjust. Many take such an attitude, but it is shortsighted, because no two people are exactly alike. They respond in different ways to different management techniques. To treat two secretaries the same way is to ignore the individuality of the current secretary. The relationship that is developed with such an attitude will not be as meaningful or as fruitful as one in which some effort is made.

All of us need recognition for our accomplishments, including secretaries, and although it may come as a news flash to many, executives also need a pat on the back once in a while. Secretaries rightfully feel indignant if the executive doesn't show his appreciation on occasion. But the same secretaries seldom think to show the executives some appreciation, or make mention of an action they took that the secretaries felt was clearly outstanding. They think that because executives outrank them, they somehow don't need the same thoughtfulness secretaries need.

In many situations, the boss enjoys a kindness too. I have known secretaries who are upset because their bosses don't show appreciation as often as they require. The thought never occurs to them to show their bosses any appreciation. "That was a thoughtful letter you dictated to Mr. McCarthy over at Bendix. It should mean a great deal to him." This is merely an example of the type of statement a secretary can make. As long as it's sincere and comes from the heart, it will be appreciated.

Many employees, including secretaries, are reluctant to compliment their boss, because they're afraid it'll be misunderstood and the boss will think they're trying to butter him up. As long as the statement is sincere and honestly felt, why hold it back? If we want kindness and thoughtfulness from others, we should begin by giving it to them. Thoughtfulness is one of those rare commodities where the more you give away, the more you're likely to receive. If this is so, why are all of us so reluctant to be thoughtful? Even if it's not returned in equal measure, there's a great amount of personal satisfaction to be achieved by knowing you are a decent, thoughtful, and humane person.

There's nothing wrong with having a high regard for yourself. As an executive secretary you are a major part of the organization. Be so competent at your job that you know in your heart that the company is better off because you've chosen to be affiliated with it. You have to hope that your boss and others in the organization will recognize it, too. It may take them longer to discover and appreciate your contribution, but they will.

It seems to me there aren't as many people interested in being executive secretaries as there once were. This is understandable, because other opportunities have been made available. It doesn't change the fact, however, that secretaries are still essential to the smooth functioning of an organization. I believe it will always be so. Word processing systems may come and go, but they'll never design a machine or a system that will take the place of an executive secretary. A system that could perform the multitude of duties required of an executive secretary hasn't been invented and isn't likely to be, as the cost would be astronomical; and you'd still end up with a system unable to make sound and quick judgments. There won't be a system or a machine that can anticipate an executive's needs, know how to interpret a scrawled message on a routing pad, or read his mind. I know companies that could survive very well without several junior executives, but couldn't make it without a couple of key executive secretaries.

Now that fewer people want to be executive secretaries, more and more companies are beginning to appreciate how valuable they are. Salaries are starting to increase and to be commensurate with the responsibilities.

The executive secretary position provides an opportunity to be involved in a wide variety of major responsibilities in the organization. The executive secretary is not a spectator; she's a participant in most of the meaningful processes taking place. She's involved early in the planning process. She has the opportunity to witness an idea being converted into an action that may have a major impact on the organization. She may be aware of recommended board policies long before the board of directors sees, considers, and acts upon them. She has the chance to learn how it all fits together and what makes it all work.

The opportunity is there. The executive secretary can have an impact on other human beings, not only through the work of the executive who employs her, but also in her own right. Being able to have a major impact on the lives of others is life's most interesting and meaningful challenge. My best to you as you accept that challenge.

Index

automobile transportation, arranging, 115, 118–119

behavior, personal, 35–36
birthdays, use of advance file system to record, 40
Boerne, Ludwig, on change, 126
business trips
itinerary for, importance of preparing, 120
preparing work material for, 119–121
see also travel arrangements
buzzers, use of, 25

calendar
appointments and, 29
recording meeting dates on, 48
card file, as integral part of advance file system, 38
career development, management positions and, 191–200
change
adapting to, as responsibility of secretary, 127
introducing, 129–133
perfectionism and, 128–130
checks, processing, as measure of trust, 71–72
closed period, 22
coffee
serving in meetings, 54–56
serving visitors, 110–111
committee meetings, 47–48
minutes of, 49–50, 56–58
see also meetings
common sense, secretary's need for, 201
communication
daily meetings as aiding, 30
informal, 27–28
two-way, 26, 27–28
community activities, as task for job description updating, 177
competition, secretary's with boss, 7

confidant
importance of, 68–69
maintaining loyalty through use of, 78
use of, in career development, 195–196
confidential letters, 19
processing of, as task for job description updating, 178
confidentiality, 45
cross-training and, 62–63
importance of, 66, 73–74
procedures to ensure, 67–69
of salary, 69–72
towards office personnel, 72–73, 152–154
see also loyalty
correspondence
use of file system for, 41
see also dictation, mail
courage, as characteristic of secretary, 3–4
courtesy, need for, with visitors, 110, 113
co-workers
authority and, 83–87
confidentiality towards, 72–73
gossip of, 67–69
credibility, importance of establishing, 72–73
cross-training
as task for job description updating, 177
use of, to avoid indispensability, 62–65

dead storage file, 138, 139
degree, college, as affecting employment opportunities, 186–197
descriptions, job, *see* job descriptions
desk manual
use of, 61–62, 65
detail, attention to, as responsibility of secretary, 126